VORACIOUS

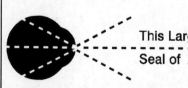

This Large Print Book carries the
Seal of Approval of N.A.V.H.

VORACIOUS

A HUNGRY READER COOKS HER WAY THROUGH GREAT BOOKS

CARA NICOLETTI

Illustrations by Marion Bolognesi

THORNDIKE PRESS
A part of Gale, Cengage Learning

Farmington Hills, Mich • San Francisco • New York • Waterville, Maine
Meriden, Conn • Mason, Ohio • Chicago

GALE
CENGAGE Learning®

LIBRARY OF CONGRESS CATALOGING-IN-PUBLICATION DATA

Names: Nicoletti, Cara, author.
Title: Voracious : a hungry reader cooks her way through great books / by Cara Nicoletti.
Description: Large print edition. | Waterville, Maine : Thorndike Press, a part of Gale, Cengage Learning, 2016 | © 2015 | Thorndike press large print Lifestyles
Identifiers: LCCN 2015037185| ISBN 9781410485946 (hardcover) | ISBN 1410485943 (hardcover)
Subjects: LCSH: International cooking. | Cooking in literature. | Large type books. | LCGFT: Literary cookbooks
Classification: LCC TX725.A1 N526 2016 | DDC 641.59—dc23
LC record available at http://lccn.loc.gov/2015037185

Published in 2016 by arrangement with Little, Brown and Company, a division of Hachette Book Group, Inc.

Printed in Mexico
1 2 3 4 5 6 7 20 19 18 17 16

To Noodle and Mummo:
For trusting my crooked path

CONTENTS

9

PREFACE

Growing up in a family of butchers and food lovers, I was surrounded by the sights and sounds and smells of cooking from an early age. But the truth is that I fell in love with cooking through reading, and I learned quickly that being in the kitchen offered me the kind of peace that settling in with a good book did. For the first half of my life I used both activities as a way to draw inward and escape from a world that I often found overwhelming. I connected deeply to the characters in my books, and cooking the foods that they were eating seemed to me a natural way to be closer to them, to make them as real as they felt to me.

I cooked and read my way through awkward middle school years, first love, devastating heartbreaks, loss, and change. As I grew older, though, reading and cooking became the forces that broke me out of my shell, allowing me to form strong relationships and connect to the world around me.

I moved to New York City in 2004 to study literature at NYU, and I quickly found myself working in restaurants, first as a server and a barista, and eventually as a line cook, baker, and butcher at some of Brooklyn's best-loved spots. Studying literature and working in kitchens, I was, for the first time, surrounded by people who loved books and food as much as I did, and it awakened me to the fact that the connection between food and literature is one that is felt deeply by many, many people.

In the locker rooms of the restaurants where I worked, I noticed my coworkers' backpacks spilling over with well-worn novels. It turned out that Hemingway and Faulkner, Morrison and Plath, were part of their lives, too, comforting them the way they comforted me, through long days of oven burns and broken emulsions. While preparing for service, picking herbs, and par-cooking fillets, we talked about short stories we had recently read and everyone's own half-written coming-of-age novel. Eating dinner at the apartments of my English-major friends, I was pleasantly surprised by how well prepared all of the food was, and how seamlessly the conversation switched from new books to new cast-iron skillets.

On my friends' bookshelves, next to the obvious college-student staples like *Moby-Dick* and *Ulysses,* sat well-thumbed volumes of *Mastering the Art of French Cooking* and *The Omnivore's Dilemma.* In between writing their own poetry and personal essays, they were bussing tables and running food, making coffee and selling high-end chocolates in restaurants and shops all over New York.

In 2008 I started a literary supper club out of my tiny, sweltering apartment, with the goal of bringing my friends' best-loved literary meals to life. When I could no longer keep up with the demand for the dinner parties, I started the blog Yummy Books, and through the success of Yummy Books, *Voracious* was born.

While doing research for this book, I took a trip home to spend some time with my childhood books. It had been many years since I had read most of them, and I felt oddly nervous on the bus ride to Boston, in the way you might feel waiting to meet a friend you haven't seen since you were small. Would we even recognize each other? When I got home I went straight up to the attic, where I spent the rest of the day and most of the night surrounded by my old friends. I was amazed at how well I still knew them, how reading them — even hold-ing them and studying their covers — transported me back to specific moments in my life with startling immediacy. What struck me most, though, was how many of them had their food scenes marked up with purple pencil, their back covers scrawled with imagined recipes. I had forgotten how long ago my fascination — my *obsession* — with food scenes in books had started.

Hosting literary dinner parties, developing recipes inspired by books for my blog, and writing this book have reinforced for me the profound connection between eating and reading. And along the way I've discovered, to my delight, how deeply this connection is felt by so many of you.

■ ■ ■ ■

PART 1
CHILDHOOD

■ ■ ■ ■

Little House in the Big Woods
BREAKFAST SAUSAGE

The playground of my childhood was vastly different from that of my peers. A few days a week, my mom would drop me off at my grandfather's butcher shop, Salett's, to do my homework and spend the hours between school and dinnertime out of her hair. Under the watchful eye of Betty the cashier, my cousin and I would play a high-adrenaline rendition of hide-and-seek we called "Get Down! Get Down!" — which involved ducking behind hanging beef carcasses in the warehouse-sized refrigerator and crouching beside buckets of rendered pork fat, fingers pointed like guns at imaginary bad guys and piles of lamb shanks.

On most days, though, I sat curled up on milk crates behind the cash register, devouring book after book while my grandfather, in his blood-spattered white coat, brought me snacks like corned cow's tongue on Wonder Bread and chicken liver pâté spread thick on Ritz Crackers. When he kissed me his cheeks were always cold from hours spent in the cutting room, a room that all the grandkids called "the stinky room" but that he somehow emerged from smelling like Calvin Klein Obsession.

I never really took an interest in what my grandfather and his brother, Bobby, were doing in the cutting room until second grade, when I began reading the Little House series by Laura Ingalls Wilder. I got the full set all at once from the Scholastic book fair at my school. I was so taken by their covers' pastel-checkered borders and colored-pencil drawings of cherubic homesteader children that I rearranged an entire corner of my bedroom in order to properly display them. The books were wildly popular with the girls in my class at that time, and many of them took to playing "Little House" at recess. I didn't find the game nearly as thrilling as the books, partially because of the humiliation of always being forced to play Pa Ingalls (in fairness, my bowl cut did make me the only viable candidate for the role).

One day, while playing the game, I pretended to walk in the door with a dead pig slung over my shoulder, ready to cut up for dinner, just as Pa Ingalls does in *Little House in the Big Woods.* The girls were horrified. "This book is from a *long* time ago," they said. "People don't do that anymore." I was mortified, mostly because I knew that people — *my* people — did indeed still do that.

After school that day I paid close attention to my grandfather and great-uncle — the fluid dance of carrying in the pigs from the truck and the focused silence that came once the animals were all on the cutting table, the way their hands changed position on their knives at the same time, in perfect choreography, and I felt proud. I watched as the pigs turned into smaller and more recognizable parts, flipping back through passages in the book for reference — "There were hams and shoulders, side meat and spare-ribs and belly. There was the heart and the liver and the tongue, and the head to be made into headcheese, and the dishpan full of bits to be made into sausage."

I saw the bin of tails and briefly imagined asking my grandfather for one to fry over the fire as the Ingalls girls did, but the thought made my knees weak, so I decided to focus on the sausage instead. We ate a lot of sausage in my house growing up, pulling it from the freezer where it was packed in bulk in my grandpa's black-and-white checkerboard bags. He made only three kinds: a spicy Italian, dotted red with paprika and cayenne; a sweet Italian, studded with plump fennel seeds; and a liver sausage that my dad wouldn't allow past our doorstep. After reading *Little House in the Big Woods* I asked Papa if he would make breakfast sausage like Ma Ingalls made, "seasoned with salt and pepper and with dried sage leaves from the garden."

I knew my grandpa loved breakfast sausage from our semi-frequent trips to Bickford's Pancake House. He always ordered a side of them with his western omelet and drowned them in that viscous maple syrup, cutting them up with the side edge of his fork rather than picking them up and eating them in two bites as my dad did. Despite how much we all liked them, my grandpa never made them at Salett's. Sage was expensive, and he already knew what his customers wanted to buy — it would have been a waste if nobody bought them, and avoiding wastefulness was the entire purpose of sausage in the first place. He was correct, of course, so the shrink-wrapped logs of Jimmy Dean that my dad always got from the supermarket to sate his craving for breakfast sausage continued to fill our freezer.

Today I work in a butcher shop with more than eighty varieties of sausages. They are packed with cheese and piles of finely diced herbs, pickled vegetables, wine, and toasted spices. I teach sausage-making classes to people who are passionate and knowledgeable about the subject, and every time the class sells out I am amazed by how much things have changed since I was a kid. Yet even with all of these varieties available, breakfast sausage remains one of my favorites.

LITTLE HOUSE IN THE BIG WOODS

Breakfast Sausage

Like Ma Ingalls's, this version uses only salt, sage, and loads of black pepper, but it also includes a healthy dose of good maple syrup, which makes all the difference in the world.

Makes 20 (4-ounce) sausage patties

5 pounds ground pork shoulder
2 1/2 tablespoons kosher salt
3 1/2 teaspoons freshly ground black pepper
1 1/2 teaspoons dried sage
1/4 cup pure maple syrup
1/4 cup ice-cold water

Place the ground pork shoulder in the bowl of an electric mixer fitted with a paddle attachment. Turn the mixer to the lowest speed and add the salt, pepper, and sage. Mix for exactly 1 minute (set a timer!). Add the maple syrup and mix for another timed minute, then add the ice-cold water and mix for one more timed minute.

Form the sausage mixture into 4-ounce patties and fry them over medium heat in a well-seasoned skillet for about 5 minutes per side.

Note: If you aren't going to cook all of the sausage patties right away, you should freeze them. Because the sugar content in the maple syrup is so high, the sugars will ferment over the course of about 3 days, causing the sausage to taste sour if you leave it in the refrigerator — which is why cooking immediately or freezing is your best bet. Stack the patties between layers of parchment paper before sealing them in a zip-top plastic bag. Frozen patties will keep for up to 6 months.

"Hansel & Gretel"

GINGERBREAD CAKE WITH BLOOD ORANGE SYRUP

In the annals of books that upset and terrified me, *Grimms' Fairy Tales* is surprisingly absent. It would make a heck of a lot more sense if this collection of creepy and horribly violent stories had kept me up at night as a kid, but for some reason I simply couldn't get enough of them. In third grade I discovered a dusty old copy of the book in my attic while snooping around after school with my best friends, Christie and Meg. We were heavily into mysteries and ghost stories at the time, and when we found the book we were certain that we had discovered some dark secret that my parents had tried to keep under lock and key.

The book was wonderfully old, with gilded pages and illustrations covered by thin sheets of onion paper, full of beautiful words like "dearth" and "soothsayer" and "earthenware." From then on, every chance we got, we snuck up to the attic, settled on some old packing blankets, and read it by flashlight.

In reality, my parents had gotten the book as a gift from a distant relative after my older sister was born and had stashed it in the attic, thinking (with very good reason) that it wasn't well suited for bedtime reading. The only real memory I have of this relative is being forced to sit on her lap at a family gathering when I was very little and her telling me, "If you don't brush your hair, your thumbs will fall off!" so it's not surprising that she was the one who gave my parents the book. *Grimms' Fairy Tales* are full of children meeting violent ends — losing limbs or getting lost in forests or being eaten by witches or wolves — but they are also full of food.

Jacob and Wilhelm Grimm knew well what it was like to want for food. Although they lived comfortably for the first few years of their lives, by the time they reached their teens they had been orphaned and left to care for their younger siblings. While compiling their collection of fairy tales they often ate only one tiny meal a day in order to make sure that their brothers and sisters were properly fed, so it makes sense that food would figure so powerfully in almost all of their stories. It is either overly abundant or absent completely; it heals and destroys, taunts, teases, nourishes, and saves; but it is always part of the narrative.

After reading a few tales, Christie, Meg, and I always found ourselves terribly hungry and, often, while eating graham crackers and peanut butter and drinking ice-cold milk, we felt vaguely guilty thinking of the starving characters we had just read about. It was conveniently close to Christmas when we reached the story of Hansel and Gretel. We had smuggled up to the attic a few Christmas decorations that we thought our parents wouldn't miss and switched from reading by flashlight to reading by electric Advent candle.

All three of us had read an edited, child-friendly version of the story at some point in our lives, which made the discovery of the original version all the more shocking. We were disgusted by Hansel and Gretel's father, so willing to kill his own children at his horrible new wife's bidding, and incensed that he got off scot-free in the end. The scene that shocked me the most, though, was the one in which Hansel and Gretel discover the witch's house and immediately begin to devour it with abandon, not even pausing when the old woman appears and yells that someone is eating her house! I was raised to respect adults, and I was horrified at Hansel and Gretel for being so piggish and rude to the old lady, witch or not.

We decided that the only way to rectify this horrid misdeed was to build our own versions of the witch's house, so Christie, Meg, and I began drawing enormous, intricate blueprints for the ultimate gingerbread house. Meg's included spiral staircases and balconies with frosting icicles hanging from them, Christie's had colorful stained-glass sugar windows, and mine featured pink spun-sugar clouds suspended above the house and a pistachio-pudding swamp. When we actually went to build our houses, we discovered that we were going to have to pare things down considerably.

In the end, we decided to pool our efforts into making one grand house rather than three. We drew and cut and traced, both on paper and on dough, editing and reworking our original ideas, chatting about the fairy tale as we mixed and rolled and waited for things to cool. It was not unlike many professional kitchen experiences I would have years later, bouncing ideas off fellow cooks, drawing and measuring, dreaming huge and then simplifying, simplifying, simplifying. Hours later, eyes bleary and fingers cramped, we stood back to look proudly upon our crooked masterpiece. Even though our stomachs were grumbling and our noses were full of the aromas of molasses and cloves, we didn't eat an inch of it, not one broken corner.

I have always found it frustrating that gingerbread houses — which are glorious in their complete edibleness — are not meant, really, for eating. You toil and sweat, smelling good smells and touching sticky dough and mixing sweet icing for hours and your only reward is *visual*. It seems so wrong. This gingerbread cake is superior not only because it is actually meant for devouring but also because it is serious and grown-up and dark, which is how I think the Brothers Grimm would have wanted it to be. The blood orange syrup pairs perfectly with the cake's heavy spicing, and it looks creepy to boot.

"HANSEL AND GRETEL"

Gingerbread Cake with Blood Orange Syrup

This cake is delicious right out of the oven but gets even better over the course of a few days.

Serves 8

2 cups all-purpose flour
2 tablespoons ground ginger
1 1/2 teaspoons baking powder
1 teaspoon ground cinnamon
1/4 teaspoon kosher salt
1/4 teaspoon ground nutmeg
1/4 teaspoon ground cloves
1/8 teaspoon ground cardamom
1 cup unsulphured molasses
1 cup stout (such as Guinness)
1/2 teaspoon baking soda
12 tablespoons (1 1/2 sticks) unsalted butter, melted
1 firmly packed cup dark brown sugar
1 cup granulated sugar

3 large eggs
Blood Orange Syrup (recipe follows)

Preheat the oven to 350°F. Spray a Bundt pan thoroughly with nonstick cooking spray. (A 6-cup Bundt pan will yield a taller cake; a 9-cup Bundt pan will yield a shorter cake.)

Sift together the flour, ginger, baking powder, cinnamon, salt, nutmeg, cloves, and cardamom in a large bowl and set aside. Combine the molasses and stout in a heavy-bottomed saucepan and bring to a boil over medium-high heat. Remove the pan from the heat. Whisk the baking soda into the molasses-stout mixture and set aside.

Pour the melted butter into the bowl of an electric mixer fitted with a paddle attachment. Add both sugars to the butter and beat until smooth. Add the eggs, one at a time, and beat until fluffy. Alternate adding the dry ingredients and the molasses-stout mixture to the butter mixture, mixing just until everything is incorporated.

Pour the batter into the greased Bundt pan and bake until a toothpick inserted into the center of the cake comes out clean, 40 to 50 minutes. Allow the cake to cool in the pan for at least 10 minutes before turning it out onto a cake stand or plate. Drizzle the cooled blood orange syrup over each piece of the cake immediately before serving.

Blood Orange Syrup
Makes about 2 cups

1 cup sugar
1 cup water
Zest and juice of 2 blood oranges

Combine the sugar and water in a sauce-pan and heat over medium heat until the sugar dissolves. Add the blood orange zest and juice and bring to a boil; boil gently for 10 minutes. Strain the syrup and allow it to cool completely.

In the Night Kitchen

SCALDED AND MALTED MILK CAKE

In February 2010 everything went wrong. In the midst of a million other inconveniences and true emergencies, I was laid off from my job as a baker at a small restaurant and suddenly unable to find work anywhere. November to February had flashed by in a frenzy of late-night Thanksgiving and

Christmas party orders — hundreds of pumpkin and pecan and apple pies, gift baskets of spicy molasses cookies, and the occasional *bûche de Noël,* and then, suddenly, silence.

I had clung to my job through a month of post-holiday lull, but eventually I came in to work one day to find a big red slash through my name on the schedule, the eyes of my fellow bakers filled with apology and relief that they had escaped my fate. I tried hard not to take it personally. I was, after all, the most recent hire, so it was only fair that I be cut first. I packed up my tools and folded my apron and walked out of the restaurant's cozy warmth and into the bracing cold of February in Brooklyn.

Unable to face going home and telling my boyfriend and sister — both of whom were struggling to find work at the time — that I had been laid off, I kept walking. I was certain that in some restaurant somewhere, a baker with a bad attitude had just ripped off her apron and stormed out, vowing never to sift or knead or frost again. I would arrive just in time to save the day, and it would be as if I had never even lost my job at all.

This, of course, didn't happen. Not even close. Every owner of every restaurant I walked into told me the same thing — that they were already overstaffed, that they also were in the post-holiday lull, that all they needed was the chocolate bread pudding that their chef always made. It was around nine at night when I finally admitted defeat and headed home. Passing by an industrial building a few blocks from my house, I noticed for the first time the smell of yeast and sugar wafting through the warehouse's open gate. I peered in the windows and saw at least a dozen Hasidic men crouched over enormous sixty-quart mixers and leaning against baking racks, white shirts tucked in over big bellies, tightly curled *payot* grazing their ears. They talked and laughed and worked, fogging up the windows with steaming loaves of bread.

I considered for half a second that maybe I was hallucinating after walking around all day on an empty stomach, that maybe I was so desperate for a baking job that I had actually just willed this place into being. I marveled that all of this hustle and bustle had been happening nearly every night right under my nose, without my ever knowing it. But what really had me rubbing my eyes in disbelief was the uncanny resemblance this secret place bore to the one in Maurice Sendak's *In the Night Kitchen.*

My parents often read *In the Night Kitchen* to me before bed when I was a kid, and I was always fascinated and slightly terrified by it. After they tucked me in, I would stare at the drawings, trying to make sense of them — a scruffy, naked boy falls into a ten-foot-tall bottle of milk and gets stirred into hot cake batter by a group of swarthy chefs, then emerges from a mixing bowl drenched in a cake-batter suit that looks much like Max's pajamas in *Where the Wild Things Are.*

In the Night Kitchen features a little boy named Mickey, who dreams that he falls out of bed and into the world of "the night kitchen" — a secret nighttime place where all of the pastries in the world are created while the rest of us sleep. A place like the one I passed by that night and, I'm sure, much like places Sendak himself probably passed many times as a child growing up in a Jewish section of Brooklyn. *In the Night Kitchen* remains, to this day, one of the most controversial children's books ever published — it is challenged and banned every year for a variety of reasons. Some critics take offense at Mickey's seemingly unnecessary nudity, some at the "phallic" milk bottle and the milky substance that makes the boy's nudity seem less pure. Some even hint at a possible World War II substory, calling attention to the chefs' "Hitler-esque" mustaches and their attempt to bake Mickey into a cake.

In 2011 I heard an interview with Sendak on NPR's *Fresh Air* with Terry Gross, in which he talked about a particularly memorable fan letter exchange, and it has stuck with me, tumbling around in my head whenever I feel particularly eager to create a recipe. The fan — a little boy named Jim — sent Sendak a "charming card with a little drawing on it," so Sendak responded in kind, sending Jim a card with a drawing of a Wild Thing. To this, Sendak got a response from Jim's mother, telling him: "Jim loved your card so much he ate it." Sendak told Gross, "That to me was one of the highest compliments I ever received. He didn't care that it was an original Maurice Sendak drawing or anything. He saw it, he loved it, he ate it."

The experience of loving something — particularly a book or a book's illustration — so much that you actually want to eat it is a sentiment near and dear to my heart. It is essentially what I'm trying to express in this book. Sendak works the idea into *Where the Wild Things Are* when the Wild Things threaten Max with "Oh please don't go — we'll eat you up — we love you so!"

Sendak's upbringing was not an easy one. Raised in Brooklyn by poor Jewish immigrants, he was a sickly and anxious child, aware from a young age that he was gay. His childhood in the late 1920s and early 1930s was haunted by war, death, economic collapse, and seemingly endless violence against children. The kidnapping of the Lindbergh baby was particularly disturbing to young Maurice, and it later factored into a few of his books. His stories are full of nightmares — children are always vulnerable and threatened by danger. Adults are either suffocating his characters with their love or disappearing completely. His characters are obstinate and often downright bratty; they defy their parents' directions and end up hurtling into danger and adventure, usually to end up — much to everyone's relief — back in their own beds again.

Growing up, I loved Sendak's books for this very reason. Parents fear that their children will be shaken up by something they read or see or hear, but these stories — the ones that get your brain working and your heart pumping — are the stories that make you realize the power of the written word, that make you fall in love with reading. They are the ones you remember most vividly, that comfort you when you're fully grown, roaming the nighttime streets of your neighborhood like one of Sendak's wandering children, peering in windows, jobless and defeated and scared for a thousand grown-up reasons.

IN THE NIGHT KITCHEN

Scalded and Malted Milk Cake
Serves 8

14 tablespoons (1 3/4 sticks) unsalted butter, at room temperature
3/4 cup granulated sugar
1/4 cup firmly packed dark brown sugar
1 vanilla bean, seeds scraped out and pod reserved
1/2 cup whole milk
2 large eggs plus 1 large egg yolk
1 1/2 cups cake flour
1/4 cup plus 1 tablespoon malted milk powder
2 teaspoons baking powder
1/4 teaspoon kosher salt

Glaze
1 1/2 cups confectioners' sugar
3 tablespoons vanilla malt powder
1 teaspoon pure vanilla extract
1 1/2 tablespoons whole milk or heavy

cream, or more if needed
1/8 teaspoon kosher salt

Preheat the oven to 325°F. Spray a Bundt pan thoroughly with nonstick cooking spray. (A 6-cup Bundt pan will yield a taller cake; a 9-cup Bundt pan will yield a shorter cake.)

Combine the butter, both sugars, and the vanilla bean seeds in the bowl of an electric mixer fitted with a paddle attachment and beat on medium speed until the mixture is light and fluffy, about 3 minutes.

While the butter is being creamed, pour the milk into a heavy-bottomed saucepan and add the vanilla bean pod. Heat the milk over medium heat, whisking constantly, until the milk reaches 180°F. Right before it reaches this temperature, you should see bubbles forming along the pan's edge and steam rising from the surface of the milk. Once the milk reaches 180°F, remove the pan from the heat and set it aside, leaving the vanilla bean pod in the milk to steep.

Add the eggs and yolk to the butter-sugar mixture, one at a time, beating well after each addition and scraping down the sides of the bowl to make sure everything is combined.

In a separate bowl, whisk together the cake flour, malted milk powder, baking powder, and salt.

Remove the vanilla bean pod from the scalded milk. With the mixer on low, alternate adding the dry ingredients and the scalded milk to the butter mixture until everything is incorporated — be careful not to overmix.

Pour the batter into the greased Bundt pan and bake until a toothpick inserted into the center of the cake comes out clean, about 45 minutes.

Cool the cake in the pan on a wire rack for 45 minutes before turning it out onto the rack to cool completely.

Whisk all the glaze ingredients together in a small bowl until smooth. If the glaze is too thick to pour, add another teaspoon of milk or cream. Pour over the cake once it has cooled to room temperature.

Nancy Drew
DOUBLE CHOCOLATE WALNUT SUNDAE

I was primed to be the biggest Nancy Drew fan of all time when I received a stack of the first ten books for Christmas in fourth grade. The year before I had read *Harriet the Spy* eight times, and as a result refused to wear anything but wide-leg orange pants and striped thermals or eat much besides tomato and mayo sandwiches. The great-aunt who had bought the Nancy Drew books for me was in her mid-seventies and had written on the inside cover of *The*

Secret of the Old Clock, in shaky but elegant script, that she had very fond memories of the series from her girlhood and that I was in for a great treat. I was so excited to get up to my room and crack open those books that at Christmas breakfast I barely even touched the icing-slathered Pillsbury cinnamon bun that I had been anticipating all year long.

For ten days straight I read a book every day, and each night after turning off my light and burrowing under the covers, I lay awake trying to figure out why I wasn't more enthusiastic about them. Nancy was smart, she was brave and daring and charismatic — she was everything I should have wanted in a female protagonist — and yet somehow she seemed hollow. Instilled with a sense of duty to my great-aunt, who had gone to the bookstore and lovingly picked them out for me, though, I pushed on and finished the ten books, feeling more and more irritated and baffled with each one.

Unlike Harriet, who was very stubbornly her own person, Nancy was *everygirl,* imbued with talents and virtues so varied that any little girl could find her relatable. This was the Stratemeyer Syndicate's aim for the Nancy Drew series — to teach little girls that they could be anything and everything, that they could be *perfect* — smart, brave, fashionable, beautiful, kind, and a darned good cook and house manager to boot. It was a noble goal, and one that girls like me, who grew up never questioning that we could be whoever and whatever we wanted, should be forever grateful for, but when I was a young reader, the idea of striving for that level of perfection only stressed me out.

Perhaps for this very reason I felt immense relief when Nancy's chum Bess Marvin entered the picture in the fifth book, *The Secret at Shadow Ranch*. Unlike Nancy and George Fayne, who seem almost compulsively eager to fling themselves headlong into dark alleys with shadowy old men, Bess is anxious and cautious, with all of the appropriate reservations of an ordinary person. While much is made of Nancy's "trim figure," and George is described as "an attractive tomboyish girl," Bess is introduced as "slightly plump" — a description that precedes her name in nearly every sentence for the remainder of the book.

As a young reader I always aligned myself with the tomboyish character in a book — Jo March, Scout Finch, Caddie Woodlawn — but in this case, I found myself immediately on Bess's side, protective of her because she was the easy target, the underdog, the brunt of under-the-table knee jabs and covert eye rolls from Nancy and George. George may be a tomboy, but unlike the tomboyish characters I loved, she is mean-spirited, always drawing attention to how much Bess has eaten and how slowly she's moving, while Nancy giggles demurely in the background.

The girls are differentiated not only by their physical appearances, but also by their relationship to food. Food is everywhere in these books, and the way that each of the girls reacts to it is telling of their personalities. Nancy loves to cook (and is, of course, fantastic at it) but cares hardly at all for the end product. Her restraint is epic. She is forever doing things like frosting warm cakes with chocolaty icing but not licking the spoon, and telling Bess and the hungry cowboys that they have to have graham crackers for dessert instead of cake. George is indifferent toward food; she often forgets to eat, and when she does it is only out of absolute necessity. She is always the one making fun of Bess for how much she eats, correcting her on the number of sandwiches she's consumed or tormenting her by saying things like "Eating is really a very fattening hobby, dear cousin." Bess is driven and consumed by food; she is constantly "starving" or "famished" or "hungry enough to eat a fried rock."

When we first meet Bess, the three girls are at a diner discussing the mysterious happenings at Shadow Ranch. Nancy and George order soft drinks while Bess studies the menu and declares that the mystery has her so upset she has lost her appetite, before adding, "I'll have a double chocolate sundae with walnuts." At this, "Nancy and George grinned. 'Poor girl,' said George, 'she's wasting away.' Bess looked sheepish. 'Never mind me,' she said." These sundaes are Bess's favorite food. They follow her throughout the series and are almost always eaten while Nancy and George smirk and sip their sodas.

The shame and general weirdness surrounding food in the series bothered me even as a child. I thought about the books for years afterward, wondering every time I saw them on bookshelves if I was the only kid who had reacted this way toward them. It wasn't until I was in college and writing a research paper on eating disorders in literature that I decided to do some research on critical receptions and feminist readings of Nancy Drew.

My first shocking discovery upon delving into Nancy Drew's complicated history was that the "author," Carolyn Keene, was not in fact a real person at all but just a made-up name created by Edward Stratemeyer. The books were actually written by a number of ghostwriters, who were paid a flat fee for their work and required to sign away all royalties and recognition to the Stratemeyer Syndicate. I was also surprised to find out that the original books had been completely rewritten starting in 1959 in order to rid them of racially insensitive language, and also to update them so that they would appeal to a modern audience. This meant that the Nancy Drew I knew was completely different from the Nancy Drew that my great-aunt was familiar with.

The original Carolyn Keene was Mildred Benson, who wrote twenty-three of the first thirty books in the Nancy Drew series. Edward Stratemeyer hired Benson to revive the failing Ruth Fielding series and was so pleased with her work that he asked her to write a new series about a girl detective that would be like a Hardy Boys for girls, and would feature an "up-to-date, modern young lady." It took me a long time to track down the original twenty-three Nancy Drew books, but once I did I could see why my great-aunt had loved them so much. Benson's Nancy, while still good at almost everything, is much more likable. She knows how to handle a rifle and wrangle horses, she is confident without the cocky condescension of the later texts, and somehow her bravery feels truer and less like a compulsive death wish.

What's most interesting about these original books compared to the rewrites, though, is how differently Bess is portrayed — and how differently the role of food figures into the narrative. In the original *Secret at Shadow Ranch* there is no mention of Bess's weight. Instead, the introduction states, "Elizabeth was noted for always doing the correct thing at the correct time. Though she lacked the dash and vivacity of her cousin [George], she was better looking and dressed with more care and taste." There is no mention of double chocolate walnut sundaes, no snarky remarks about Bess's eating habits. Rather, all of the girls seem to have healthy appetites in the original *Secret at Shadow Ranch.* They are equally tantalized by "the odor of hot biscuits, chicken sizzling in butter, and fragrant coffee," washing up quickly so they can sit down to "a table which fairly groaned with plain but delicious food."

As glad as I was to read a version of the text that wasn't so fraught with food anxieties and shame binges, I was sad to see the double chocolate walnut sundaes go, if only because I knew how much Bess enjoyed them. I never eat a sundae without thinking of Bess, and I eat sundaes more often than I should admit (I am an independent woman and I can do whatever I want). This recipe is my ode to Bess, my favorite underdog. It has milk chocolate ice cream covered in a thick, warm chocolate sauce that tastes as close as I could get to the Brigham's fudge sauce I was raised on, and it's topped with candied walnuts with a healthy pinch of salt and a kick of cayenne.

NANCY DREW

Double Chocolate Walnut Sundae
Prepare the milk chocolate ice cream, candied walnuts, and chocolate fudge sauce (recipes follow). Once all of your components are ready, create your sundae by layering the ice cream and candied walnuts in an ice cream dish and topping with the hot fudge.

Milk Chocolate Ice Cream
Makes about 1 quart

1 1/2 pounds good-quality milk chocolate,

roughly chopped

2 cups heavy cream

2 cups whole milk

1 vanilla bean, seeds scraped out and pod reserved

1 pint (16 ounces) stout (such as Guinness), boiled until reduced to 8 ounces

8 large egg yolks

1 cup sugar

1/2 teaspoon kosher salt

Prepare an ice bath by filling the sink or a very large bowl with ice cubes and cold water. Place the chopped chocolate in a large glass or metal bowl and set it aside, along with a fine-mesh strainer.

In a large, heavy-bottomed pot, whisk together the cream, milk, and vanilla seeds and pod over medium heat until the mixture is just about to boil (you will see small bubbles forming around the edge of the pot and steam rising from the surface of the liquid). Whisk in the reduced stout and remove the pot from the heat.

In a large bowl, combine the egg yolks, sugar, and salt and whisk vigorously until fluffy and light, about 3 minutes.

Remove the vanilla bean pod from the scalded milk mixture and discard. Transfer some of the scalded milk to a 1-cup glass measuring cup. Slowly pour it into the yolks in a steady stream, whisking constantly. Continue to do this until all of the scalded milk is incorporated into the egg yolks.

Pour the yolk and scalded milk mixture back into the pot and cook over medium-low heat, whisking constantly, until the mixture reaches 170°F. Pour the mixture through the strainer into the bowl of chopped milk chocolate and whisk until the chocolate has melted and is incorporated throughout.

Set this bowl containing the ice cream base on top of the ice in the ice bath and whisk until it cools slightly. Allow it to cool over the ice bath, whisking occasionally, until it reaches room temperature, about 20 minutes. Cover the bowl and transfer it to the refrigerator to chill for at least 8 hours.

When the base is thoroughly chilled, spin it in an ice cream maker according to the manufacturer's instructions. Allow the spun base to set up in the freezer for at least 2 hours before serving.

Candied Walnuts
Makes about 1 cup

1/2 cup sugar
2 tablespoons water

Pinch of cayenne
1 cup toasted walnuts
1 teaspoon flaky salt (such as Maldon)

Spray a baking sheet with nonstick cooking spray and set aside.

Combine the sugar, water, and cayenne in a small, heavy skillet. Cook over medium heat, undisturbed, until the sugar begins to melt, about 4 minutes. Continue cooking, occasionally stirring gently, until the sugar caramelizes to a deep amber, about 2 more minutes. Remove from the heat, quickly add the walnuts to the caramelized sugar, and toss to coat. Spread out the sugar-coated walnuts on the greased baking sheet, using a fork to separate any that are sticking together. Sprinkle them with the flaky salt and allow to cool for about 10 minutes.

Chocolate Fudge Sauce
Makes about 1 1/2 quarts

1 2/3 cups sugar
1 cup plus 2 tablespoons Dutch process cocoa powder
1 cup water
1 cup corn syrup
1 cup (2 sticks) unsalted butter
8 ounces good-quality semisweet chocolate,

chopped
3 tablespoons pure vanilla extract
Pinch of kosher salt

Combine all of the ingredients in a heavy-bottomed saucepan and heat over medium heat, whisking occasionally, until the sauce comes together. Serve warm. Leftovers can be stored in a covered container in the refrigerator for at least 3 months. Reheat before serving.

IF YOU GIVE A MOUSE A COOKIE

BROWN BUTTER CHOCOLATE CHIP COOKIES

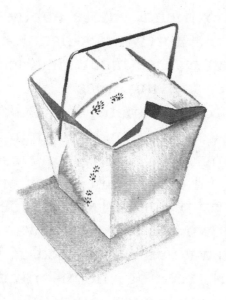

My second year at NYU I was living in Chinatown in a small apartment with five other students. The building was nestled cozily between a criminal court and a homeless shelter, just steps away the frenetic chaos of Canal Street. The second week of September, my roommates broke the news to me that they had all decided to study abroad during second semester. I left the apartment to walk to class, and a homeless man threw up Cheetos-colored vomit on my open-toed shoes, as if to say, "Abandon all hope, you silly nineteen-year-old."

In January I found myself living with four strangers, including a meek young woman whom I never, not once, heard utter a word, and her boyfriend, whose hobby was knife throwing. He threw thick-handled knives at the kitchen wall all night long, leaving gaping, plaster-spewing holes.

The third roommate was a six-foot-four celebrity-obsessed med student who was always singing a creepy song called "I'm My Own Grandpa" under her breath. She used to camp out in front of the popcorn factory down the street and wait for them to throw away industrial-sized garbage bags filled with reeking, neon-orange cheese popcorn, which she would then lug home to the apartment and eat, noisily, late into the night.

Finally, there was a tiny, hunched art student whose oily black curls were forever hanging over her face and who once barked at me when I begged her to throw away the takeout food she had been collecting in her bedroom. When I say "barked" I don't mean that she got snippy with me, I mean she actually opened her mouth and let out a dog bark so unnervingly realistic it still gives me chills to think about it.

What I'm trying to tell you is that this was a very lonely time for me.

One night, shut in my bedroom watching reruns of *Dynasty* on my laptop, I saw out of the corner of my eye the tiniest, sweetest-looking little mouse sitting on his haunches staring at me. I'm sure he was lured into the apartment by the smell of my room-mate's putrefying egg foo yong (or maybe it was the cheese popcorn), but for some reason I found his company immensely comforting. For the next few nights I waited patiently for him to reappear and he always did, twitching his nose in the blue light of my laptop screen. When he suddenly stopped visiting I panicked. Images of glue traps flashed through my head and, in a moment of sheer desperation (and extreme loneliness), I crumbled a piece of the chocolate chip cookie I was eating, placed it on the floor where he usually sat, and waited. A few minutes later he appeared and I, the only person ever to have this reaction upon seeing a mouse in her apartment, let out a giant sigh of relief.

A few weeks later the apartment was over-run with mice. They crawled up through the burners on the stove and huddled in the corners of the cabinets under the sink. When the guy I was dating at the time asked how in the hell things had gotten so out of control I admitted to him what I had done on that lonesome night. He was astoundingly angry at me. "YOU ACTUALLY *GAVE* A MOUSE A COOKIE?! HOW COULD YOU DO THAT? DID YOU NEVER READ THE BOOK?!"

We broke up shortly after that.

The thing is, I *had* read the book — many, many times. It was a bedtime staple at my house, and one of my all-time favorites. Despite the fact that the book has been panned by many a critic and author (most famously by Maurice Sendak, who replied simply, "UGH!" when Stephen Colbert asked him about it), I maintain that it is a valuable piece of literature. As a kid I liked the book for the delicious illustrations and the precious, overalls-clad mouse. As an adult I like it for its sinister message — if you ever give anyone anything they will always ask for more.

I am convinced that the author, Laura Numeroff, was an embittered counter-girl at some upscale Manhattan coffee shop before she struck gold with *If You Give a Mouse a Cookie*. Laura, like so many of us who have struggled trying to please the general public, knows that if you give a customer a free coffee, chances are she is going to ask for it to be a latte, soy, no foam, extra whip, two pumps, extra-hot but room temp.

I think about the book on a daily basis, and whenever one of my coworkers freezer-packs a single sausage for a customer and ends up, forty minutes later, breaking down fifteen cuts of meat to grind an eighth of a pound of custom burger, I always think, "You gave that mouse a cookie."

While visiting my parents' home recently I found my old copy of the book, and like so many other books from my childhood, it had a dreamed-up recipe written in my round kid handwriting on its back cover. The recipe was for my (and every kid's) favorite cookie — chocolate chip — crisp, chewy, and fluffy all at once. I've updated these cookies to suit my adult taste buds, browning the butter first and adding a healthy sprinkling of flaky salt.

Brown Butter Chocolate Chip Cookies
Makes 2 dozen cookies

2 1/4 cups all-purpose flour
1 teaspoon kosher salt
1 teaspoon baking soda
1 cup (2 sticks) unsalted butter, browned and cooled to room temperature so that it is solid again, but soft
1 cup firmly packed light brown sugar
1/2 cup granulated sugar
2 teaspoons pure vanilla extract
1 large egg plus 1 large egg yolk
1 cup good-quality semisweet chocolate chunks
Flaky sea salt (such as Maldon), for sprinkling

In a medium bowl, whisk together the flour, salt, and baking soda and set aside.

In the bowl of an electric mixer fitted with a paddle attachment, beat the brown butter and both sugars on medium until light and fluffy, about 3 minutes. Add the vanilla and beat until incorporated.

With the mixer running, add the whole egg and beat until it is mixed in, and then add the yolk and beat until it is mixed in.

Slowly add the flour mixture, being sure to pause and scrape down the sides of the bowl, until everything is incorporated.

Add the chocolate chunks and beat until they are evenly spread throughout.

Scoop the cookies and lay them on a sheet pan covered in parchment. (The dough is very hard to scoop after it sits in the fridge.) Refrigerate the dough balls for at least an hour (if you can bear to wait even longer, chilling the dough overnight produces the best results).

Once the dough is chilled, preheat the oven to 350°F. Line two baking sheets with parchment paper or silicone baking mats and arrange the balls on them so there is at least 1 inch between each cookie.

Sprinkle the dough balls with flaky salt. Bake until beautifully golden brown, 12 to 15 minutes.

Eat immediately or allow the cookies to cool on a cooling rack.

THE INDIAN IN THE CUPBOARD
GRILLED ROAST BEEF

Long before *Toy Story* came out it was common knowledge around the Nicoletti household that our toys came to life when we left the room. Looking back, I have a sneaking suspicion that my mom's stories about the secret life of her Papa Bear might have been a ruse to get us to take better care of our toys — which, admittedly, worked like a charm. Papa Bear was my mom's favorite stuffed animal when she was a child, and he was a legend in our house. She had seemingly endless stories about catching him moving around when she was pretending not to look — scratching his ears or snuggling farther under the blanket. He had been loved to the point of being completely furless, one shiny black eye hanging precariously from a thread, giving him an adorably deranged smirk. My sisters and I took turns sleeping with him, and we always made sure he was somewhere comfortable before we left for school. We even memorized the position we left him in, so that we could spot if he had moved while we were gone.

There was never any question in our minds that all of our toys had a rich secret life. We wondered constantly what their personalities were really like, which ones were fighting, and which ones were in love. Every day before school my older sister, Ande, would announce to all of the toys in our room that although we were leaving and would be back later, they didn't have to stop doing what they were doing when we got home. They were safe, she told them, and we would never tell anyone that they were really alive. After school we would creep up to our bedroom as quietly as possible and fling open the door, hoping to catch a glimpse of the world of our imagining, but it was always frustratingly out of reach. I still remember the fear in my friend Hannah's eyes when I told her excitedly that her favorite teddy bear was in fact alive. And it must be said that the thought of some of our toys coming to life — particularly our troll dolls and a large alien figurine that my dad called "the it" — was unsettling. There were nights that I lay awake, convinced that I heard the trolls shuffling around, plotting revenge for that time I put them all in tiny toilet-paper diapers.

Some of the most popular and enduring children's movies and books of all time feature toys coming to life — from *Toy Story* to *Corduroy* to *The Velveteen Rabbit* — proof that my sisters and I weren't the only kids who harbored this fantasy. Of all the books in this vein, Lynne Reid Banks's *The Indian in the Cupboard* was by far my favorite. My mom and her twin sister read it to my cousin Cam and me the summer before second grade, and to this day it remains one of my most vividly remembered reading experiences. To me, the most thrilling element of the book was the fact that Omri, the protagonist, got to live out every imaginative child's fantasy — the one that we played out over and over again when we sat our stuffed animals at the breakfast table, or forced cake into their fur mouths at tea parties and bedroom-floor picnics — the fantasy of getting to *feed* your most beloved toys.

Much of the book's beginning is centered on Omri's quest to meet Little Bear's digestive demands. At first he is flummoxed by what to feed the toy he has brought to life: "What did Indians eat?" he asks himself. "Meat, chiefly, he supposed, deer meat, rabbits, the sort of animals they could shoot on their land." Unfortunately for Omri, his British cabinets are filled only with "biscuits, jam, peanut butter, that sort of thing." When he finds a can of corn, he's relieved, having learned in school that Native Americans grew and harvested corn. The canned corn is far from what Little Bear is used to. He's so tiny he has to hold one single kernel with both hands. He is skeptical at first, "turning the corn around in both hands, for it was half as big as his head." Eventually, though, "he smelled it. A great grin spread over his face. He nibbled it. The grin grew wider."

Little Bear's biggest demand is for meat to cook, and Omri comes up with the genius idea of building him a meat-spit from his

Erector set. Little Bear isn't used to using a spit, but "he soon got the hang of it. The chunk of steak turned and turned in the flame, and soon lost its raw red look and began to go gray and then brown," and before you know it the bedroom is filled with "the good juicy smell of roasting beef."

Cam and I were awed by that meat-spit, and we begged our parents to let us build one of our own over one of the enormous bonfires we frequently had in the summer. The closest we got, though, was watching our moms prepare roast beef for our enormous family. Because the summers were oppressively hot and our house wasn't air conditioned, our moms always cooked the roast on the grill out back. Cam and I would pull up chairs next to the grill and watch as they seared it off, thrilled every time the fat dripped and caused the flames to flare up. While we waited for the roast to cook, we peeled back ears of sweet summer corn, rubbing off the silk and checking for worms, and we talked about Omri and Little Bear and the cowboy Boone. When the roast came off the grill to rest, the corncobs went on, wrapped back up in their husks. On these nights we sat down to eat feeling exultantly close to Omri, Little Bear and his wife, Bright Stars, and Boone, as though we had made something of our own come alive.

THE INDIAN IN THE CUPBOARD

Grilled Roast Beef
Serves 6 to 8

2 tablespoons olive oil
2 tablespoons kosher salt
1 tablespoon coarsely cracked black pepper
1 tablespoon crushed red pepper (optional)
Finely chopped leaves of 2 rosemary sprigs
4 garlic cloves, pressed through a garlic press
1 (3- to 4-pound) boneless strip loin roast,
    fat trimmed to 1/4 inch

Mash together the oil, salt, black pepper, red pepper (if using), rosemary, and garlic, rubbing the mixture together with your fingers to distribute the ingredients throughout. Rub the mixture all over the roast and let it sit at room temperature for about 45 minutes. (For best results, wrap the seasoned roast and refrigerate it overnight; just be sure you allow it to come back to room temperature before cooking the next day.)

Preheat the grill on high.

When the roast is ready and the grill is hot, place the roast on the hottest part of the grill, close the lid, and sear until a good crust starts to form and the meat releases from the grate easily, 5 to 8 minutes per side. (If you have a standard charcoal grill, make one side of the grill hotter by piling more coals on that side, and sear the meat on that side.)

Once the meat is seared, turn the heat down to let the beef roast, fat-side up. (If you have a three-burner grill, place the roast in the middle and turn that middle burner off. If you have a four-burner grill, turn the middle two off and place the roast there. If you have a charcoal grill, simply move the roast to the cooler side of the grill.) Place a cabled instant-read thermometer into the thickest portion of the roast and close the lid. If there is a thermometer on your grill telling you the grill's temperature, it should be between 300°F and 350°F.

Let the roast cook until the instant-read thermometer reads 125°F to 130°F for medium-rare, 30 to 40 minutes.

Remove the roast and let it sit for at least 10 minutes before carving it against the grain and serving.

THE BOXCAR CHILDREN
CHOCOLATE PUDDING

When I was in elementary school, on days when it was too rainy for us to go outside for recess, our teachers would gather us in the library and pull down a giant, yellowed projection screen to watch movies. This should have been the most exciting thing in the world for a seven-year-old, but our librarian always insisted on playing the 1978 animated rendition of *Puff the Magic Dragon*. Maybe it was the only movie she had, or maybe she loved it, but I cannot describe to you how much I hated this movie. Not only did the entire premise of it terrify me, but it gave me the saddest, most anxious feeling deep in my gut, a feeling that stayed with me for days afterward, with those dulled psychedelic colors and Peter, Paul, and Mary's eerie crooning creeping into my nightmares. I had a vague notion that Jackie Paper, with his wide, wet eyes and terribly fragile name, was sick or dying — it was all too much.

Finally, there came a day when the rain was blowing against the windows of my first-grade classroom and, panic mounting at the thought of recess, I worked up the courage to ask my teacher, Miss Walker, if I could please do something else during the movie screening. When we all filed into the library that afternoon, Miss Walker ever so quietly pulled me out of the herd and took me over to the bookshelves. "Pick a book and you can read quietly until the movie is over," she said with a secretive wink. To this day, that memory remains one of the happiest of my childhood — not only because I had escaped Puff, but because of Miss Walker's infinite and quiet understanding, and her gift to me of thirty minutes surrounded by books.

The book I chose that day, and for many, many days afterward, was the first installment of the Boxcar Children series, a book originally written by first-grade teacher Gertrude Chandler Warner in 1924. The series has been continued by various writers over the years, and there are now more than a hundred Boxcar Children titles. The first book remains one of the most beloved children's books of all time ninety years later, and with good reason — it's packed with action and adventure and smart, lovable characters. The stories follow the Alden children — Henry, Jessie, Violet, and Benny — who have been orphaned. Threatened with the prospect of being separated, the children set off on their own, creating a home inside an abandoned boxcar beside a river.

The books caused quite a stir at first. Parents objected to the children's happy, adult-free world and the tragic backdrop of their story — all very real, scary stuff. Yet somehow I never once felt upset by the Alden children's misfortune (this coming from a girl who was destroyed by a magical dragon). Warner, like my own Miss Walker, knew children well, and because of that she wrote about them well. The tragedy that the Alden children face is overshadowed by their resilience and never once puts a damper on their adventurous spirit and curiosity.

The Alden children are hungry for life and for food, and Warner writes about both kinds of hunger brilliantly. The first glimpse we get of the children is of them standing in front of a bakery window, staring longingly at the baked goods and deciding whether to spend what little money they have on bread or cakes. The rest of the book, and all of the books that come after, is full to the brim with food. Between solving mysteries and getting into trouble, the children cook and eat the most tempting-sounding foods: brown bread with cheese, blueberries and milk, fragrant beef stew simmered in a tin kettle over an open fire, and cherry slump eaten underneath cherry trees.

One treat that comes up over and over in the books is chocolate pudding — a dessert that has always been near and dear to my heart. Every Thursday night when I was a kid, my mom would make us chocolate pudding while we watched *The Simpsons*. She always used My-T-Fine brand cook-and-serve pudding mix, and I never tired of standing by the stove and watching it turn from chocolate powder and milk to a thick, creamy pudding. My sisters liked to have theirs chilled in the fridge first, and Ande

70

would always put a layer of plastic wrap directly on top of hers to make sure it didn't form that icky skin, but I liked mine still piping hot, a layer of the ice-cold heavy cream my dad used in his coffee poured generously on top.

Among many other things, *The Boxcar Children* taught me that pudding didn't always come from a package, that it could actually be made from scratch — a notion that bewildered and absolutely thrilled me. Inspired by the Aldens' competence in the kitchen, I tried for years to make a chocolate pudding from scratch that tasted as good as or better than the boxed version I knew so well. I failed many, many times, scorching the bottom of the pudding, or ending up with raw cornstarch, gluey textures, and scrambled eggs hidden under chocolate chunks. Still, in keeping with the Boxcar Children's resilient spirit, I pushed on. Twenty years later I finally have a chocolate pudding recipe that I love, and whenever I eat it (still steaming hot and doused with cold cream) I think of the Alden children in their tiny boxcar kitchen, young and hungry and, against all odds, happy.

Chocolate Pudding
Serves 6

2 cups heavy cream
1 cup whole milk
1/2 cup sugar
1 vanilla bean, seeds scraped out and pod
  reserved
3 tablespoons unsweetened cocoa powder
1/4 teaspoon kosher salt
5 egg yolks
3 tablespoons cornstarch
4 ounces good-quality semisweet chocolate,
  chopped
2 ounces good-quality milk chocolate,
  chopped

In a medium saucepan combine the heavy cream, milk, sugar, and vanilla seeds and pod. Cook over medium heat until steam starts to rise from the surface and tiny bubbles appear at the edge of the pan. Whisk in the cocoa powder and salt until smooth.

In a large bowl, whisk the egg yolks and cornstarch until they form a thick, smooth paste. Slowly and carefully pour the hot milk mixture into the yolk mixture, whisking vigorously the entire time, until fully incorporated. Return the mixture to the saucepan and cook over medium heat, stirring constantly, until thick and creamy (if you have a thermometer it should be at 180°F).

Place all of the chocolate chunks in a heat-safe bowl and pass the hot custard through a fine-mesh strainer over the chocolate. Mix and fold until the chocolate melts into the custard and is smooth and shiny. Eat immediately or refrigerate, pressing plastic wrap flush to the pudding's surface first to prevent a skin from forming.

PIPPI LONGSTOCKING
BUTTERMILK PANCAKES

When I was six, my older sister and I were playing Dog School and I split my eyelid open. Oh, you don't know what Dog School is? Dog School consisted, quite simply, of my sister Ande and me pretending we were dogs — crawling around on all fours, barking, panting, and generally irritating my mother to no end. When my sister tired of the game (or, more specifically, of me) she would herd me into the bathroom, otherwise known as "Dog School," with our real dog, an enormous yellow Lab named Nate, and barricade the door so that we couldn't get out.

I had to stay in there for a long time in order to learn all of the doggish things that all dogs need to know — or at least until my mom got wind of the whole thing and let me out. One night, Nate grew restless and, in an attempt to escape, jostled me into a table. I went into it face-first, splitting the skin just below my eyebrow and leaving me banging on the door screaming to get out with blood gushing down my face.

After some tears and quite a few stitches, I was sent home from the hospital with a big black patch over my eye, looking like the tiniest, saddest pirate ever. The worst part was that my dad had finally gotten us tickets to "Disney on Ice" the next night — an event that my sister and I had been begging to see for months. The TV commercials for it were relentless, airing seemingly every ten minutes. Each time Mickey and Princess Ariel glided past us on the screen we both let out a little whimper of helpless longing, and our determination to see them grew stronger. What a cruel and terrible fate that when I finally got to see this majestic display I could only *half* see it.

I squinted with my one good eye all night, trying desperately to see everything. This, combined with all the cotton candy I ate, left me with a searing headache. By the time I got home I was in full meltdown mode, sick and disappointed and overstimulated (so many sequins!). In an attempt to calm me down, my dad found a copy of *Pippi Longstocking* and, thinking that maybe the stories of her pirate father might make me feel better about my patched eye, tucked me into bed and began reading it to me.

Some advice for all parents out there: if you have a kid who is already overwrought and anxious, Astrid Lindgren's *Pippi Longstocking* is not the book you should read to her. Ande, ever the party girl, was thrilled by the book, laughing aloud and kicking her feet at Pippi's brazenness and spontaneity, but I was horrified. Her unpredictability bewildered me — her life was an unstructured nightmare, a circus! And I hated circuses. Even her appearance terrified me — those untamed flaming red pigtails, that cavernous gap in her garish smile. In the same way that Amelia Bedelia frustrated me with her constant mess-ups, and Guy Smiley's inability, on *Sesame Street,* to control his voice sent me into a panic, Pippi's chaotic existence had me stressed.

The only thing I found redeeming about Pippi was her cooking prowess. Pancakes were Pippi's specialty. She even had a song she would sing while she was making them, for which my dad made up a tune: "Here pancakes will be baked now / Here pancakes will be served now / Here pancakes will be fried now!" When Pippi cracked the eggs from high above the bowl and flipped the pancakes way over her head, then topped them with sugar and served them with a side of brown sausages or pineapple pudding, it made me despise her a little bit less.

The morning after "Disney on Ice" I woke up ravenous for pancakes, which were not often served at our house. There was cereal for breakfast, donuts if we were lucky, and lots of Pop-Tarts and toaster strudels, but who has time, with three young kids, for pancakes? Surprisingly, though, my mother obliged my request and together we cracked eggs and sifted flour, and she taught me how to watch for the ring of bubbles around the edge of each pancake that lets you know that it's time to flip.

We talked about the book as we cooked, and I asked my mom how she would feel if a girl like Pippi were to move in next door.

She told me she wouldn't like it very much, and that she understood why Pippi made Tommy and Annika's mother (and me) so nervous. Lost in the rhythm of my mother's whisking, all of the anxiety I had felt over the past few days over my eye, and "Disney on Ice," and Pippi Longstocking evaporated. It's one of my favorite memories — a moment when I felt very close to my mother.

Years later, faced with the prospect of having to make fifty quarts of pancake batter for a single brunch shift at the Brooklyn restaurant Colonie, separating hundreds of eggs and whisking quarts of egg whites to stiff peaks, folding them into batter until my arm felt as if it would fall off, I remembered that morning with my mother, talking about a book and finding peace in the rhythm of the kitchen, and I instantly felt calmer. The result was the best pancake I ever made — crisp at the edges and fluffy inside, not too sweet and not too buttermilk-tangy — it's a pancake that I think even Pippi would approve of. And though I can't stand her, this is important to me.

Buttermilk Pancakes
Makes 12 to 15 pancakes

6 large eggs, separated
3 1/3 cups full-fat buttermilk
2 teaspoons baking soda
3 cups all-purpose flour
2 tablespoons sugar
4 teaspoons baking powder
1 teaspoon kosher salt
6 tablespoons (3/4 stick) unsalted butter,
　browned and cooled slightly
Butter and pure maple syrup, for serving

In the bowl of an electric mixer fitted with a whisk attachment, whisk the egg yolks on medium until pale yellow and very smooth, about 3 minutes. With the mixer still running, add the buttermilk and baking soda and whisk until well incorporated. In a medium bowl, whisk together the flour, sugar, baking powder, and salt, and slowly begin adding this dry mixture to the running mixer. When all of the dry ingredients are incorporated, add the browned butter and whisk until the batter is very smooth.

Transfer the batter from the mixer to a separate bowl. Rinse the mixer bowl, dry it, and add the egg whites. Whip with the whisk attachment until stiff peaks form. Gently fold the egg whites into the batter until they are incorporated.

Let the batter settle for 15 to 20 minutes before frying on a very hot griddle. Serve warm, with butter and maple syrup (or brown sausages and pineapple pudding).

ANNE OF GREEN GABLES
SALTED CHOCOLATE CARAMELS

When I was six years old, my dad's dad, my Grandy, passed away after weeks of refusing to eat. He had been sick in a vague and insidious way ever since my grandmother died years before I was born. There was a subtle but persistent ache in his chest that no doctor could diagnose. When asked how he was feeling he always answered the same way — he rolled his eyes back in his head and dragged his hand across his chest until it rested, fingers splayed out over his heart. As young as I was and as sick as he got, my memories of him are still startlingly clear, and in them he is always tall and strong and silly.

The night of his wake, my parents left my sisters and me at his apartment with a babysitter, a stranger in a floral muumuu who immediately put on a rerun of *Donahue* and distractedly fed us Apple Jacks from Grandy's cupboard. Grandy had an upstairs neighbor, a woman named Lila who was around his age and who always brought him peanut butter cookies. Grandy hated peanut butter, but he never had the heart to tell her, so his cabinets overflowed with Lila's peanut butter–filled, peanut-studded cookies. We ate them whenever we came to his house, armfuls of them. They were good cookies, chewy and salty, each one pressed with fork tines in a crisscross pattern. I think she loved him.

That night she must have heard the TV on in his downstairs apartment, and she came to the door, knocking gently with her finger, holding a Tupperware container of cookies. When she asked for Grandy, the babysitter announced loudly, too loudly, that he had died. I remember there was a sound of physical pain, like someone being socked in the stomach or a dog getting his foot stepped on, and suddenly the cookies were in the babysitter's hands and Lila was backing away from the door, glassy-eyed and trembly.

The babysitter, unfazed, poured milk into jelly jars and placed the container of cookies in front of us. My mouth was watering from the warm smell of them, but there was a pain in my throat, an actual lump that made the thought of eating unimaginable. I kept thinking about Lila alone upstairs in her apartment, the sound she had made, and the wild, stricken look of sorrow that had washed over her face. My throat felt so tight, the lump in it so enormous and painful, that I started to panic, and I cried until the babysitter tucked me into bed in Grandy's guest room, where I stared at a smudged chalkware bust of the Virgin Mary — her eyes crazed with grief — until I fell asleep.

I had no idea how to process the choking sadness I had felt that night until I started reading *Anne of Green Gables* two years later. In the third chapter, Anne, who is grappling with the reality that Marilla and Matthew don't want her, tells Marilla that she can't eat breakfast because she is "in the depths of despair." Her explanation of this phenomenon was so strikingly similar to what I had experienced the night of Grandy's wake that I remember actually gasping aloud as I read it. "It's a very uncomfortable feeling indeed," Anne says.

When you try to eat a lump comes right up in your throat and you can't swallow anything, not even if it was a chocolate caramel. I had one chocolate caramel once two years ago and it was simply delicious. I've often dreamed since then that I had a lot of chocolate caramels, but I always wake up just when I'm going to eat them. I do hope you won't be offended because I can't eat. Everything is extremely nice, but I still cannot eat.

Realizing that your emotions and experiences aren't yours alone is one of the great powers of reading, especially when you're a child. The feelings that I hadn't been able to pinpoint or understand were there on the page in front of me, and I was both awe-struck and comforted. As melodramatic as Anne often is, her feelings here are real, and they speak to the incredible power that grief has over appetite.

L. M. Montgomery's food writing is legendary, especially in the Anne of Green Gables series — which includes raspberry cordial, vanilla ice cream and lemonade, plum pudding with vanilla sauce, pound cake and raspberry tarts, coconut macaroons — but these unswallowable chocolate caramels are, to me, the most powerful. In a book that so often tumbles toward the slapstick and ridiculous, this scene is a tiny glimpse into the tragedy and sadness that this eleven-year-old girl has experienced — tragedies not dissimilar to those in Montgomery's own life.

On Wednesday afternoons when I was in elementary school, my neighborhood friends and I would walk to Andrews Pharmacy and sit on the carpet beneath the magazine racks, doing quizzes from teenybopper magazines and eating chocolate until our stomachs cramped. Christie always chose milk chocolate buttercreams and I always picked the gold-wrapped cherry cordials that gushed liquid so sweet it stung my throat. When our friend Lisa came she always chose chocolate caramels, big, chunky squares sunk deep in paper wrappers. I can still hear Lisa's laugh as she bit down on one end and pulled the sticky sugar up, up into the air, thin spiderwebs of caramel clinging to the tip of her turned-up nose.

It was right before Christmas 2012 when my sister called to tell me that Lisa had passed away after battling cancer for a little over a year. In what was either a massive cosmic coincidence or some kind of comforting wink, I was in the middle of rolling and enrobing a thousand chocolate candies for a wedding when I got the call. The restaurant was too warm to roll truffles without melting them, so I had been standing in the walk-in refrigerator, shivering under a puffy parka for hours, melted chocolate stuck deep beneath my fingernails, cocoa powder coating my hair and eyebrows in a dull mist. I felt that familiar lump in my throat, that choking, alarming sadness, that stomach-twisting gut punch. I cried with my whole body alone in the fridge, my hands still working in a flurry of angry energy. I cried until my throat loosened and my mouth uncramped, thinking about Grandy and Anne and those Wednesday pharmacy visits, about Lisa and Lila and grief so palpable it sticks in your throat like burned sugar.

I left the walk-in and set up an induction burner. I unwrapped the good salted butter from its gold foil wrapper and cut it into even cubes. I weighed dark brown sugar and measured the thick, heavy cream. I warmed my hands over the pot, watching as the mixture thickened and boiled to a creamy fragrant amber, stuck my spoon into the caramel, and pulled it away from me, up, up into the air.

ANNE OF GREEN GABLES

Salted Chocolate Caramels
Makes about 80 caramels

1 1/2 cups heavy cream
1 1/3 cups granulated sugar
1/2 cup firmly packed dark brown sugar
1/2 cup light corn syrup
3 tablespoons unsalted butter
3 tablespoons salted butter
Seeds of 1 vanilla bean
1 1/2 pounds good-quality semisweet chocolate, chopped
2 teaspoons flaky sea salt (such as Maldon)

Grease an 8-inch square glass baking dish. Cut a piece of parchment paper so that it is a little bit less than 8 inches wide by 14 inches long. Press the parchment into the baking dish, leaving 3 inches of paper hanging over the sides of the dish (this will make it easier to lift the cooled caramel out of the baking dish). Coat the parchment in more butter and set the baking dish aside on a metal cooling rack.

In a large, heavy-bottomed saucepan, bring the cream to a boil over medium-high heat. Stir in both sugars and the corn syrup. Bring this mixture back to a boil and cook, stirring constantly, until the sugars have completely dissolved, about 3 more minutes.

Reduce the heat and continue to gently boil the mixture until it reaches 255°F on a candy thermometer. Don't worry if the temperature rises quickly to 225°F and then plateaus for a little while — this is normal. It should take 20 to 25 minutes for the mixture to reach 255°F.

Once the mixture has come to temp, remove it from the heat and add the un-salted and salted butters and the vanilla bean seeds, stirring until combined. Pour this mixture into the prepared baking dish and allow it to cool on the cooling rack until the surface is set and the baking dish is warm but not hot, about 1 hour.

At this point, transfer the dish to the refrigerator to chill for 15 minutes (don't leave it in there longer than that!). After 15 minutes, run a knife along the edges of the baking dish and use the parchment paper ends that are hanging over the dish to carefully lift the caramel out of the pan.

Line two baking sheets with parchment paper. With a very sharp knife, cut the caramel into 3/4-inch squares, set them on one lined baking sheet, and place them in the refrigerator to continue to harden while you temper the chocolate.

Set up a double boiler: Fill a medium saucepan with 2 inches of water and bring it to a simmer over medium heat. Place a heat-safe glass bowl over the pot and add two-thirds of the chopped chocolate, stirring until the chocolate has melted and a candy thermometer registers 118°F. Remove the bowl from the double boiler and add the remaining chopped chocolate, stirring until the temperature of the chocolate reaches 80°F.

Return the 80°F chocolate to the double boiler and bring it back up to 88°F (it's important that the chocolate stay between 87°F and 89°F while you are enrobing the caramels, because this is the temperature at which it will set and harden to a smooth shell).

Take the caramels out of the fridge and dump them into the melted chocolate. Use a fork to remove them, one at a time, allowing the excess chocolate to drip off before placing them on the second lined baking sheet and sprinkling them with flaky salt. Make sure the caramels are not touching, and let them sit until the chocolate completely sets, about 30 minutes. The caramels will keep in an airtight container in the refrigerator for up to 2 weeks.

HOMER PRICE

OLD-FASHIONED SOUR CREAM DONUTS

Donuts have figured more heavily in my life than I would like to admit. "Donut" was one of the very first words I spoke and, perhaps because of this, my family rarely calls me by any name other than "Doozy Donuts" (although I'm still unclear on where the first part of that nickname came from). After church on Sundays, if my sisters and I had been good, my parents would take us to Dunkin' Donuts and we would each get to choose a treat. We never told them that our Sunday school teachers had already given each of us ten donut holes an hour earlier in an attempt to keep us quiet while they taught us about the Crucifixion. Once my sisters were in the store, their decisions were simple — Ande: jelly; Gemma: chocolate frosted with sprinkles — but my favorites were constantly changing. I dabbled in toasted coconut and Boston cream, strawberry-frosted and honey-dipped, lemon-filled and powdered-sugar-dusted, and I never tired of the old-fashioned, my father's favorite.

My dad's breakfast specialty hinged on the old-fashioned donut, which may be why I hold such a special place in my heart for it. In our house, there was always a box of Entenmann's old-fashioned donuts in the cabinet, and if we were lucky enough to catch my dad before he went to work, he would carefully split one in half for us, toast it, and slather it with salted butter. I casually mentioned this to a friend recently, thinking it was normal, and she was horrified, but I stand with my dad on this one. After a quick round in the toaster oven, even those packaged donuts came to life — suddenly all burned-sugar edges and bone-warming nutmeg, salty butter pooling in every imperfection that the factory had somehow failed to smooth over.

The summer I was seven years old my mom and her twin sister bought my cousin and me Robert McCloskey's *Homer Price* — a book of beautifully illustrated adventure stories from the 1940s. They would read it to us every night before bed, and I remember well the excitement that I felt when we finally got to the story "The Doughnuts." In the story, Homer is working at his uncle Ulysses's donut shop. Ulysses invents a machine that can make donuts at lightning speed. Things, of course, go awry and the machine malfunctions, spitting out donuts faster than they can sell them.

Soon the entire store is filled, floor to ceiling, with donuts (not the worst problem), and a customer's pricey gold bracelet has gone missing in the dough. The story is goofy and charming and all ends well. However, rereading it as an adult, I couldn't help but hear a bit of fear in McCloskey's voice. "The Doughnuts" was written in 1943, only nine years after a donut machine was a major attraction at the world's fair, marketed as a glimpse into our robotic future.

The fear of being replaced by machines remains with us today. It's a fear that creeps into my bones every time I read about factory butchering (or encounter an intern who is young and efficient and willing to work for free). The robotic future of McCloskey's nightmares became a reality in the realm of donuts. I never tried, or even saw, a fresh, handmade donut until I was around nineteen. I never made a donut from scratch until I started baking professionally in my twenties, and when I did start, they were the pastries that scared me the most. Over the course of time (and hundreds of failures) I learned how to mix and knead, how to fix a dud batch, and how to carefully drop the dough into the fryer without dousing myself in hot oil. Mostly I learned patience, or — as Laura, the girl who first taught me to make donuts would always say — I learned how to "become one with the donut."

Donuts have been experiencing a bit of a revival the past few years. It seems as if a new artisanal donut shop pops up in Brooklyn every other week. They're vegan, they're gluten-free, they're covered in neon frostings and pumped full of local fruit jams, they come in flavors like mojito, black licorice, grapefruit ginger, rose, root beer, and café au lait. This is all well and good (*really* good), but I will still choose an old-fashioned donut every single time.

Old-Fashioned Sour Cream Donuts

These are old-fashioned donuts for an old-fashioned story. The sour cream makes a shaggy dough that results in donuts with deep, crispy creases that absorb every bit of the glaze. The sugar is light and the nutmeg is cozy; the yeast is in there more for its flavor than its rising properties. These donuts are the toasted and buttered Entenmann's of my childhood all grown up, but they're even great without toasting or buttering. (Of course, if you want to gild the lily, please be my guest.)

Makes 2 dozen donuts and donut holes

1 cup sour cream
1 teaspoon active dry yeast
2 large eggs
1 cup granulated sugar
3 1/2 cups pastry flour
1 tablespoon baking powder
1 teaspoon nutmeg
1 teaspoon kosher salt
1/2 teaspoon baking soda
5 1/3 tablespoons unsalted butter, melted
  and cooled a bit

1/4 teaspoon pure vanilla extract
Canola oil, for frying

Glaze
1/4 cup whole milk
1/4 teaspoon pure vanilla extract
2 cups confectioners' sugar, sifted

In a small saucepan, heat the sour cream over low heat until it is very warm but not hot to touch, and mix in the yeast to dissolve. Set aside.

In the bowl of an electric mixer fitted with a paddle attachment, beat the eggs and granulated sugar until thick and light yellow, about 3 minutes.

While the eggs are being creamed, whisk together the flour, baking powder, nutmeg, salt, and baking soda in a separate bowl and set aside.

Once the eggs are thick, add the butter and vanilla and mix until well incorporated. With the mixer running, alternate between adding the dry ingredients and the warm sour cream until everything is well mixed.

Transfer the dough to a well-oiled bowl, cover loosely with greased plastic wrap, and refrigerate for at least 2 hours or up to overnight.

Line a baking sheet with parchment paper

and lightly oil the parchment. Once the dough has rested overnight, turn it out onto a well-floured surface and roll to 3/4 inch thick. Cut with a 2 1/2-inch donut cutter (or a 2 1/2-inch circle cutter for the donuts and a 1/2-inch circle cutter for the holes) and set the donuts and holes on the lined baking sheet. Gather the scraps into a ball, reroll, and cut (do this only once or the donuts will be tough).

Cover a wire cooling rack with paper towels or brown paper bags. Heat a large pot halfway full of oil to 350°F.

While the oil is heating, make the glaze. Heat the milk and vanilla in a medium saucepan over low heat until warm. Add the sifted confectioners' sugar and whisk until completely smooth. Transfer the glaze to a bowl and set it over a pot of warm water to keep it from hardening while the donuts fry.

Once the oil is up to temp, use a slotted spoon to lower the donuts two at a time into the oil. Cook until deep golden brown, 1 1/2 to 2 minutes per side. Remove the donuts from the oil with the slotted spoon and transfer to the paper towels. Once all of the donuts are fried, fry the donut holes in 2 batches and drain on paper towels. Dip the donuts and donut holes in the warm

glaze or drizzle it over them. Eat immediately.

The Witches

MUSSEL, SHRIMP, AND COD STEW

Recently, a group of friends and I were reminiscing over dinner about various childhood humiliations, swapping stories about terrible first kisses, super-flared jeans, mushroom cuts, and organized dance routines. One friend talked about laughing until she wet her pants at a middle school semiformal; another told of getting a jumbo cola thrown at her from a car full of older girls.

Then my friend Nick, who is also from Massachusetts, told us about the time he went on a class field trip to the Salem Witch

Museum in third grade and threw up from sheer terror in front of his entire class as soon as the tour guide placed his head in the stocks. I was laughing so hard I had tears coming down my cheeks, but the rest of my friends, all of whom grew up outside New England, were absolutely horrified, unable to believe that we were taught about such violent atrocities at such a young age.

I had always assumed that this was a part of everyone's elementary school curriculum — that everyone had learned about Cotton Mather and Bridget Bishop, about stonings and hangings, before being dismissed, wide-eyed and silent, for recess. I was shocked to learn that most of my friends had never heard of the Salem witch trials until high school, when they were assigned *The Crucible,* and others not until midway through college, when it came up in an Early American History class.

After that night I started asking friends who teach elementary school whether they taught their students about the witch trials, and all but one of them laughed and said that they would never be allowed to. It got me thinking about my early education and the teachers who firmly and honestly taught me and my peers about witch hunts and genocide and war. These were the blue-haired New England teachers of the old school, who wore sensible, midcalf cotton skirts and believed that fear was an integral part of educating children.

I loved these women, with their Ivory soap smells and tea-stained teeth and their willingness to tell the truth about just how ugly the world can be. It was easiest to imagine that these ladies, who never once mentioned husbands or children of their own, lived at the school — unlike those bubbly, young, just-married teachers who were forever showing us photos of their new homes and kittens and bringing their husbands to school for visits. It was also easy to imagine that these women, who insisted on teaching us about the atrocities of the Salem witch trials, were themselves witches.

Year after year rumors circulated about the same teachers, and things only got worse after we read Roald Dahl's *The Witches.* While the history lessons about the witch trials provided us with impractical tools for spotting a witch — hidden birthmarks and difficulty reciting the Lord's Prayer — *The Witches* told us that it was as easy as looking at hair, hands, eyes, gums. We looked and looked, finding signs wherever we wanted to and making them up when we couldn't.

As a child, anything that I read in a book was the absolute truth as far as I was concerned, so when Dahl told me in the foreword to *The Witches,* "This is not a fairy tale. This is about REAL WITCHES," I believed him wholeheartedly. I read the book like a manual, flipping back to it for reference whenever an adult was particularly cruel to me or an old woman looked at me for too long while I read at the library.

Dahl, like the teachers of my youth, wasn't shy about frightening children. His insistence that what he was writing was true is perhaps one of the reasons that this book has always been so controversial — kids are gullible and witch hunts are real, and teaching children to look for physical signs in a woman that will condemn her as evil is dicey territory. Before the Salem witch trials in 1692, there were the Vardø witch trials in Norway, starting in 1621 and continuing intermittently until 1663. These trials serve as the historical backdrop to *The Witches.* The narrator's grandmother hails from Oslo and assures him that "her witch stories, unlike most of the others, were not imaginary tales. They were all true. They were the gospel truth. They were history."

Besides their bleak shared history of witch hunts, Norway and Massachusetts also find common ground in the fact that they are coastal and have therefore relied heavily on the ocean as a food source throughout history. I never knew just how spoiled I was by Massachusetts seafood until I moved away from home and ate in other cities. Growing up, we consumed enormous amounts of seafood — tiny, sweet scallops and plump, briny Wellfleet oysters; mayo-heavy lobster rolls, with meaty claws peeking out from inside buttered hot dog buns.

In the winter we ate oven-broiled cod, white and flaky and covered in butter and Ritz Crackers. In the summer we rowed a rickety boat a half mile out to gather armloads of shiny, tight-lipped mussels from a gigantic lion-shaped rock, braving razor-sharp barnacles and dive-bombing seabirds so that we could have mussels, steamed or grilled, for dinner. In every season we ate steaming bowls of creamy, chest-warming clam chowder dotted with sweet corn and linguiça sausage and full-bellied littlenecks.

One scene in *The Witches* resonated with me the most, both as a child and as an adult: the one in which the narrator's grandmother reminisces about her childhood days spent "out in the rowing boat." She tells him about how she and her brother used to explore the tiny islands along the coast, diving into the sea "off the lovely smooth granite rocks," dropping anchor to fish for cod or whiting, and frying up whatever they caught in a pan for lunch — adding that "there is no finer fish in the world than absolutely fresh cod."

They used mussels for bait, and if nothing bit they would "cook [the mussels] in seawater" until they were "tender and salty" and "delicious." When they were feeling less ambitious they would simply row out to sea and wait for the shrimp boats to head home, waving at the men so that they would stop and give them handfuls of shrimp, "still warm from having just been cooked," and they would "sit in the rowing boat, peeling them and gobbling them up," even sucking out the head to make sure they got every last bit. It's a beautiful passage, and one that reminds me just how much talent Dahl had, not only as an imaginative storyteller, but as a writer.

Reading about cod and mussels and shrimp so close together immediately makes me think of the cioppino my family used to get in the Italian North End of Boston, packed with the morning's catches and simmered in wine and plump tomatoes and speckled with crushed red pepper.

Mussel, Shrimp, and Cod Stew

In this recipe I use mussels, shrimp, and cod for their literary authenticity, but feel free to add or substitute any fish or shellfish you prefer, or whatever looks the freshest at the market.

Serves 6

2 tablespoons olive oil
1 tablespoon unsalted butter
1 yellow onion, diced
1 fennel bulb, thinly sliced
1 bunch fresh parsley, roughly chopped
1/2 bay leaf
2 teaspoons kosher salt, plus more to taste
5 garlic cloves, roughly chopped
1 teaspoon crushed red pepper
1 (28-ounce) can crushed tomatoes
2 1/2 cups chicken stock
1 1/2 cups dry white wine
1/2 cup bottled clam juice
2 tablespoons tomato paste
2 fresh basil leaves, finely chopped
Leaves of 4 thyme sprigs
1 1/2 pounds mussels, debearded and washed
1 1/2 pounds large raw shrimp, peeled and

deveined (thawed if frozen)
1 1/2 pounds skinless cod fillets, cut into
  2-inch pieces
Freshly ground black pepper
Crusty bread, for serving

In a very large pot or Dutch oven, heat the oil and butter over medium heat. Add the onion, fennel, parsley, bay leaf, and salt and sauté until the onion and fennel are translucent, about 10 minutes. Add the garlic and crushed red pepper and sauté for 2 more minutes.

Add the crushed tomatoes, chicken stock, white wine, clam juice, tomato paste, basil, and thyme to the pot. Stir, cover, and cook until the mixture comes up to a simmer. Reduce the heat and continue to simmer, covered, for 30 minutes.

Add the mussels, cover, and cook until they begin to open, 5 to 10 minutes. Stir in the shrimp and cod, cover, and simmer until they are just cooked through, another 5 to 10 minutes. Discard any mussels that did not open.

Season the stew with salt and pepper to taste. Ladle into shallow bowls and serve with good, crusty bread.

THE SECRET GARDEN
CURRANT BUNS

I'll admit that I was slightly skeptical about Frances Hodgson Burnett's *The Secret Garden* when it showed up on my pillow one night before bed in third grade. My mom had placed it there, hoping I would love it as much as she did when she was my age. It was brand-new, a delicious-smelling cream-colored paperback with elegant green lettering that swirled like wild vines around a little girl in her checkered raincoat who stood surrounded by pink roses. It looked precious, and I was wary of precious.

Only a few weeks earlier I had thrown my copy of Eleanor Hodgman Porter's *Pollyanna* clear across the room in frustrated disgust, knocking over my little sister's cereal bowl and causing an outburst of crying and yelling. It was unlike me to do something so aggressive, but Pollyanna Whittier had been riding my last nerve for days, with her "glad game" and her perfect flaxen hair. As soon as I opened *The Secret Garden*, though, it was clear that Mary Lennox was no Pollyanna; this was a dark book about dark subjects — neglect and anger, grief, illness, and hunger — I devoured it quickly and thought about it for weeks after.

When *The Secret Garden* was published in 1911, the genre of children's literature was in its golden age. In the late 1800s a change occurred in how children were perceived. They were no longer viewed as tiny adults or as creatures born full of sin, but as clean slates with their own unique personalities that needed to be shaped with care and enriched with imaginative play. Authors like Lewis Carroll, George MacDonald, and Charles Kingsley wrote humorous adventure and fantasy stories that replaced the didactic and instructive children's literature of previous years. Along with this new belief in children's autonomy came fear and curiosity about what happens when children are left to grow up on their own, outside the domestic sphere and without the guidance of parents. This fear was especially prevalent in England, where the number of orphaned children far outnumbered the available spots in orphanages.

Both children's and adult literature of the mid-nineteenth and early-twentieth centuries is littered with orphans — Mark Twain's Tom Sawyer and Huck Finn; Lucy Maud Montgomery's Anne Shirley (*Anne of Green Gables*) and Emily Starr (*Emily of New Moon*); the Brontë sisters' Jane Eyre and Heathcliff; Charles Dickens's Oliver Twist, Pip, Estella Havisham, and David Copperfield; Victor Hugo's Cosette and Quasimodo; Little Orphan Annie; Heidi; and, of course, Pollyanna Whittier and Mary Lennox.

Every author of this time period had his or her own way of dealing with the orphan problem — the orphans are saved by generous benefactors, by their own positivity, by hard, honest work, by love. For Mary, it is not only the neglected garden she discovers at Misselthwaite Manor and prunes back to health that saves her, but the appetite that this physical work awakens within her. Her transformation from sour, scrawny, and embittered to empathetic, healthy, and joyful can be traced directly to what and how much she is eating.

The first meal we see Mary eat is at her home in India, during the cholera outbreak that kills her parents and most of the house staff. After being completely forgotten and shut up in her nursery for five whole days, she emerges, thirsty and starving, with no idea where anyone is. She wanders into the dining room, which she finds empty, "though a partially finished meal was on the table and chairs and plates looked as if they had been hastily pushed back when the diners rose suddenly for some reason." It is in this creepy, postapocalyptic scene that Mary scrounges up a meal of "some fruit and biscuits, and being thirsty she drank a glass of wine which stood nearly filled."

It's a sad and lonely meal, made even sadder when Mary, who is so young she doesn't really know what wine is, gets drunk and stumbles back to the nursery "frightened by cries she heard in the huts and by the hurrying sound of feet." The now-orphaned Mary is quickly swept away from the abandoned house in India and sent to live in the sprawling mansion of her mysterious uncle

Archibald Craven, whom she has never met before, in the moors of England. The next time food is offered to her, it is on her train ride to Misselthwaite Manor with the head servant, Mrs. Medlock, who presents a cozy meal of "some chicken and cold beef and bread and butter and some hot tea" in a lunch basket. Mrs. Medlock is cheered up considerably with this meal, but there is no mention that Mary eats any of it. Instead she sits and stares at Mrs. Medlock, who, after eating a great deal, falls sound asleep.

When Mary arrives at Misselthwaite Manor, however, she isn't as easily able to avoid eating without notice. When she awakes the first morning, the table in her room is set "with a good substantial breakfast. But she always had a very small appetite, and she looked with something more than indifference at the first plate that Martha set before her." In Mary's former life, no one seemed to notice if she ate or not, but Martha, the maid at Misselthwaite, is incensed and baffled by her refusal to eat her porridge, telling her "Tha' doesn't know how good it is. Put a bit o' treacle on it or a bit o' sugar." She tells her how much her brothers and sisters, who are "as hungry as young hawks an' foxes" and have "scarce ever had their stomachs full in their lives" would love to eat the breakfast that Mary is spurning, to which Mary responds, "I don't know what it is to be hungry."

After a few days spent wandering outside in the fresh air of the moors, chasing a friendly robin and poking around the walls of the garden, Mary wakes up hungry for the first time ever, and much to Martha's delight devours all of her porridge without any prodding. The more time Mary spends outside with Martha's brother Dickon, restoring life to the garden that she had found in a state of neglect and isolation similar to her own, the hungrier she becomes. Soon she's plotting ways to sneak snacks between meals and boasting to her cousin, Colin, "I'm getting fatter and fatter every day. Mrs. Medlock will have to get me some bigger dresses. Martha says my hair is growing thicker. It isn't so flat and dull and stringy."

The meals that signal Mary's final and total transformation are the ones that she, Dickon, and Colin eat in the garden. Burnett describes these garden picnics with such enthusiasm that I remember actually salivating over them as a child. There is "hot tea and buttered toast and crumpets," "home-made bread and snow-white eggs, raspberry jam and clotted cream," as well as eggs and potatoes roasted in the ground and slathered in fresh butter and salt. My favorite meal of all, though — the one that I pined for nearly as much as I pined for Dickon himself — was the "two tin pails full of rich new milk with cream on the top of it, and cottage-made currant buns folded in a clean blue and white napkin, buns so carefully tucked in that they were still hot."

When I was a child, the closest I ever came to cottage-made currant buns were the hot cross buns that appeared in my local grocery store every year around Easter, stacked high in plastic clamshells, all perfectly uniform in that conveyor belt kind of way. Even though those buns were far from homemade and never warm, I loved them, with their hard little currants and frosting crosses.

I didn't taste a homemade currant bun until a couple of years ago, when my older sister and I were living together while she was going to pastry school. After making them at school one night, she brought a box of them home and presented them to me. I nearly cried when I opened the box and saw them, all shiny and round and studded with tiny black currants. They were still warm, even after their long ride on the L train back home, and unlike the ones I had grown up eating, they were heavy with the intoxicating smell of fresh yeast and orange peel. We curled up on the couch, both of us still covered in flour from long days of pastry making, and ate the whole box.

THE SECRET GARDEN

Currant Buns
Makes 1 dozen

4 teaspoons active dry yeast
3/4 cup whole milk, warmed slightly (about 110°F)
3 3/4 cups bread flour
1/3 cup sugar
3 large eggs, at room temperature
1 cup (2 sticks) unsalted butter, at room temperature
1 teaspoon finely grated fresh orange zest
3/4 teaspoon kosher salt
1/4 teaspoon ground nutmeg
1/3 cup dried currants, soaked in warm water until plumped and softened

Glaze
1/2 cup sugar
3 tablespoons water
1 teaspoon pure vanilla extract
1/2 teaspoon finely grated fresh orange zest

In a small bowl, stir the yeast into the warm milk until it is completely dissolved, and set it aside to activate. If it doesn't start foaming within 12 minutes, discard it and try a new batch of yeast.

In the bowl of an electric mixer fitted with a dough hook, mix the bread flour, sugar, eggs, butter, orange zest, salt, nutmeg, and milk-yeast mixture on low until the dough comes together, then increase the speed to medium and knead until the dough is smooth and elastic, 5 to 7 minutes.

When the dough is nearly there, strain the plumping currants and add them to the dough, kneading until they are incorporated. Transfer the dough to a well-oiled bowl, cover it with plastic, and let the dough rise in a warm place until it has doubled in bulk, about 1 1/2 hours.

Line a baking sheet with parchment paper or a silicone baking mat. Once the dough has risen, turn it out onto a well-floured surface and divide it into a dozen even pieces. Roll the pieces into balls using the palm of your hand against the floured surface. Place the balls on the lined baking sheet, leaving about 2 inches of space between the buns.

Cover the sheet with plastic and allow the

dough to rise again for 45 minutes to 1 hour.

Near the end of the rising time, preheat the oven to 350°F. Bake the buns until they are nicely golden brown, 25 to 30 minutes.

When the buns are close to done, prepare the glaze by combining the sugar, water, vanilla, and orange zest in a small saucepan and bringing to a simmer over medium heat, stirring until the sugar is completely dissolved. Once the buns are ready, brush the glaze over the buns while they are still hot. Transfer the buns to a cooling rack and allow them to cool slightly before serving.

CHARLOTTE'S WEB
PEA AND BACON SOUP

I have to say that, on the lengthy list of the most challenged and banned books, I'm surprised *Charlotte's Web* doesn't show up more often. The book certainly hasn't gone unnoticed by teachers and parents looking to protect the innocent — it's been banned in Kansas for including talking animals, which some educators deemed "unnatural," and avoided by others who think the themes of death and sacrifice are too heavy for its young audience. It has also been challenged in England by teachers worried that the discussion of eating pork would be offensive to Muslims. My teachers, however, never gave a second thought to the repercussions of assigning this book to a butcher's granddaughter.

The popularity of *Charlotte's Web* in third grade certainly didn't do me any favors socially, and it was single-handedly responsible for turning half of my class, as well as my sisters and my cousin Caroline, into vegetarians for a short period of time. I ended up eating the bacon for all of the girls in my family that year, terrified that my grandfather would notice the strips untouched on the side of their lumberjack breakfast plates at Bickford's and start asking questions.

That year my older sister got into the torturous habit of whispering "Wilbur" into my ear whenever she saw me eating pork, a practice that never failed to bring me to the brink of tears. I loved animals desperately and dearly as a child — I still do — and this book made me feel incredibly guilty. I was nervous that my classmates would find out that my grandfather butchered pigs, or that my friends who knew would tell everyone. I was in a constant state of self-conscious paranoia.

The wave of vegetarianism that *Charlotte's Web* inspired wasn't isolated to my family members and childhood friends. I have at least one adult friend who never ate pork again after reading the book as a child. While the book didn't turn me away from meat, reading it was an enormous turning point in my understanding of the food I ate and where it came from. I knew a good deal, certainly more than most of my classmates, about what the meat I ate looked like before it was run through a grinder and neatly shrink-wrapped for the supermarket case, and I knew, logically, of course, that what I saw on the cutting room tables at my grand-father's shop had only recently been a live animal, but that was where my thought process stopped. It's hard to wrap your mind around the enormity of death when you're a child — harder, in some ways, if you happen to stare it casually in the face every day after school.

E. B. White is unapologetic about the baldness with which he talks about death in *Charlotte's Web.* From the startlingly stark first line of the book, "Where's Papa going with that ax?" White forces his young read-ers to confront an uncomfortable reality, one that he himself struggled with — that animals die for our consumption. As a child, after having read *Charlotte's Web,* I assumed that E. B. White must himself be a vegetarian. I was shocked when I started reading his essays in high school and college and learned that not only was he a meat eater, but he also raised his own pigs for slaughter.

There are two distinct voices in the book, that of Mr. Arable, who views his animals from the practical standpoint of a farmer — as property and a means of survival — and that of Fern, who views Wilbur's death from an emotional standpoint, as a terrible injustice. White himself seems to fall somewhere between these two. He connects deeply with animals, humanizing them and using them to communicate about loss and friendship and death in both his children's books and personal essays. He is also, however, a man who writes in "Good-Bye to Forty-Eighth Street" about his trip to the Fryeburg Fair, where he attends "the calf scramble, the pig scramble, and the baby-beef auction" and "enjoy[s] the wild look in the whites of a cow's eyes."

The secret guilt that I felt as a child after reading *Charlotte's Web* was still present when I reached adulthood, and I wrestled daily with questions of the ethics of my job as a butcher. Many of my vegetarian friends would ask me how I could love animals and do what I did for a living, and as often as I spouted answers back at them I still wondered, privately, if it actually was possible. Then I read White's essay "Death of a Pig," which perfectly demonstrates that eating and loving animals are not mutually exclusive, or at the very least that it's okay to be unsure about the answers to these enormous questions and that I wasn't alone in asking. In the essay, White, who had been happily raising pigs for years, finds himself "shaken to the core" over the illness and sudden death of one of his animals — a pig who had "evidently become precious" to him, and who in the end he mourned "not as the loss of a ham, but the loss of a pig," as a creature who "had suffered in a suffering world."

When White published *Charlotte's Web* in 1952, factory-farming practices were on the rise, and while there were animal protection laws in place in Europe, not many people in the United States were talking about the ethical treatment of animals, especially in connection with farming. With the Great Depression still fairly fresh in their minds, Americans were more concerned about having enough food than they were about where that food came from. White took great pride in the fact that his pigpens were comfortable and his pigs well fed and happy. He was, in many ways, far ahead of his time in his farming practices and his thoughts on sustainable, traceable food.

In "A Report in January," White talks about the new factory farm process of cleaning eggs, a process so harsh it leaves their shells looking like "a cheap plastic toy," and adds, "If that's an egg, I'm a rabbit." In "Coon Tree" he worries about the future of vegetable farming, citing a speaker he heard at the American Society of Industrial Designers who said that "we would push a button and peas would appear on a paper plate," to which he responds, "I'm not much of an eater, but I get a certain nourishment out of a seed catalogue on a winter's evening, and I like to help stretch the hen wire along the rows of young peas on a fine morning in June, and I feel better if I set around and help with the shelling of peas in July. This is part of the pageantry of peas, if you happen to like peas."

Ethical farming practices and food traceability are on everyone's minds these days — certainly I think about, talk about, read about, and hear about these issues on a daily basis. Today I work in a butcher shop that sources beautiful pastured pigs from two local farmers that we visit often. The first time I went on a farm trip it was late October and freezing rain was coming down in thick, stinging droplets. For weeks leading up to the trip I had been anxious about how I would feel seeing the animals that I knew would eventually end up on our cutting tables. When we got to the farm I stood staring at the pigs for a long while, their strong speckled backs and their busy snouts, and I was struck by the fact that I didn't feel sad. I had pictured myself, upon seeing the field of pigs, filled with the sudden, melodramatic urge to run at them with my arms flung wide, screaming apologies, snot and tears flying, but instead I just stayed quiet while the pigs snorted and squealed and croaked.

When I returned to the farmhouse, there were steaming mugs of coffee on the table, topped off with milk from the dairy cow, Lucy, that was so grassy and sweet that I didn't even need to add sugar. There were heaps of eggs, their shells blue and brown and white and their yolks nearly orange, and there was a pile of fragrant bacon made from pigs from that very farm, pigs that we had butchered and cured and smoked ourselves in the weeks before. From where I sat at the table I could see the chickens in their small red henhouse, snuggled close on their bleachers. Lucy's jaw was working over some hay in the field below us, and the pigs were rooting and rolling around just beyond us, and everything felt circular and happy and warm, and I think I forgave myself a little.

CHARLOTTE'S WEB

Pea and Bacon Soup

My first instinct was to give you a recipe for bacon, but somehow that didn't seem quite right. So I've decided to focus on E. B. White's love of peas for this recipe and provide a recipe for pea soup with an optional bacon garnish. This soup can be made completely vegetarian by substituting vegetable stock for the chicken stock and using croutons instead of bacon for crunch. If you decide to go that route, use an extra tablespoon of butter in place of the bacon grease.

Serves 4 to 6

1 tablespoon unsalted butter
1/2 cup diced cooked bacon, for garnish, 1 tablespoon bacon grease reserved
1 cup chopped yellow onion
1 leek, roughly chopped

2 garlic cloves, minced
2 teaspoons kosher salt, plus more to taste
4 cups chicken stock
5 cups fresh or frozen peas
1/2 cup sour cream or crème fraîche
Freshly ground black pepper

Heat the butter and bacon grease in a large, heavy-bottomed saucepan over medium-high heat until the butter is melted. Add the onion and leek and cook until translucent, about 7 minutes. Add the garlic and salt and cook until the garlic is lightly browned, about 3 more minutes. Add the chicken stock and bring the mixture to a boil. Add the peas and cook until tender, about 5 minutes (frozen peas will take less time).

Remove the soup from the heat and transfer about one-third of it to a blender. (*Note:* Hot soup creates steam, and this steam has nowhere to go in a blender, which can lead to scary explosions if you don't follow this tip: On the lid of your blender there should be a hole that is covered by either a cap or a wand. Remove the cap or the wand and cover the hole with a clean kitchen towel. This gives the steam room to escape, which means the hot soup won't explode all over you.)

Blend the soup in batches until it is very smooth. You can also use an immersion blender for this step if you have one, and simply blend the soup in the stockpot. For extra-smooth soup, pass it through a fine-mesh sieve after blending.

Transfer the soup to a large bowl, whisk in the sour cream, and season with salt and pepper to taste. Portion the soup out into bowls and sprinkle the crispy bacon on top.

WHERE THE RED FERN GROWS
SKILLET CORNBREAD WITH HONEY BUTTER

When I was thirteen I used to babysit for a family with two young kids and an ancient golden retriever named Sammy. Whenever I babysat, I had to complete a long and messily handwritten checklist of tasks to keep poor, ravaged Sammy alive. She was forever having accidents on the carpet and staring at me with exhausted, sorry eyes. Often I was so overwhelmed by the pill crushing and ointment spreading that I would forget to bathe or feed the kids, or I would lose track of time sautéing ground beef for Sammy's dinner and end up putting the kids to bed an hour late.

One night, I put Sammy's dinner down and took the kids downstairs to go to sleep. When I came back upstairs, Sammy was lying next to her untouched dinner, eyes rolled back, foam spilling from her mouth. Terrified and hysterical, I called the parents and they rushed home immediately. They scooped up her tired body and whisked her off to the animal hospital in their blue Volvo station wagon, and I said a little prayer that rather than getting more pills and shots, Sammy would finally be allowed to be at peace.

The relief that I felt for Sammy when she did in fact pass that night immediately disappeared when I saw how devastated the mom was. She was inconsolable when she returned home, and I felt immense guilt on the walk back to my house, a tiny part of me wondering if my small prayer had somehow caused this giant sadness.

At home I went straight up to my room and immediately dissolved into the kind of self-indulgent crying fit that only a thirteen-year-old can muster. A half hour later I pulled myself out of bed and went digging for my well-loved copy of *Where the Red Fern Grows*. All of the dog drama had reminded me of the story and I thought that maybe the book, which I had loved so much as a kid, and which tells the story of a boy who loses his beloved dog, would comfort me.

I had read it for the first time in second grade after choosing it from one of those Scholastic book fair packets they used to pass out once a year in elementary school. Was there anything more exciting than those colorful, book-filled, whisper-thin packets? I was always a sucker for any books that looked slightly spooky or adventure-packed, and I remember distinctly the third grade book fair in which I picked up *Maniac Magee, Wait Till Helen Comes,* and *Where the Red Fern Grows* based on their promising-looking covers. It was the first book ever to bring me to tears — I remember crying dramatically into my dog Henry's fur upon completing the last lines.

The book put me at ease enough to realize that I was absolutely starving, not only from the hour of full-body sobbing I had just done, but also from all of Wilson Rawls's delicious food descriptions. The farm-freshness of everything in Billy's meals was dazzling to me, both as a kid and as a teenager. Books like these had me searching my backyard for edible berry bushes, mushrooms, and roots before sitting down at night to a meal of Weaver chicken nuggets and canned fruit cocktail (no complaints, Mom, it was delicious).

One food that appears repeatedly throughout the book is cornbread — Billy stuffs it in his rucksack to go camping, he sells stale chunks of it as bait to the fishermen, he makes salt pork sandwiches between its crumbly layers, and he eats it with jarred peaches, fried potatoes, fresh huckleberry cobbler, or honey and butter. Inspired by the book and desperately wanting to clear my conscience of the guilt I felt over Sammy's death, I decided I would make a batch of cornbread for Sammy's family. Baking the cornbread succeeded in comforting me where the book hadn't, and by the time I was done cracking eggs and measuring milk I felt almost back to normal.

The next morning, I walked the cornbread over to the family's house. I was expecting that maybe in the light of day, having had the night to mourn Sammy and reflect on her long and happy life, Sammy's mom would feel better, but I'll never forget how exhausted and deeply, unreachably sad she still looked when she opened the door and saw me standing there with a tray full of cornbread squares. I felt very young and very silly when she patted my head distractedly before closing the door.

What I know now, having lost both of my childhood dogs, is that the grief of losing a beloved pet — especially one that has been in the family for many years — is as much about recognizing the passing of time and the closing of chapters as it is about mourning companionship.

I learned this firsthand when Henry died, right before I left for college. Henry was a miniature dachshund and my constant companion from the time I was seven until I was eighteen. He was a tiny, anxious thing who followed at my heels and slept on the pillow beside my face every night.

Henry loved to eat crayons so much that he even learned how to remove the paper wrappers in order to consume just the wax. At first we blamed my little sister for all the missing crayons, but then Henry started to poop the most beautiful, colorful jewels all over the yard. They were speckled with neon pinks and greens, oranges and purples — just gorgeous poops. They were so beautiful it took everything I had to convince my best friend that they weren't candy and she couldn't eat them. My sisters and I would walk around the yard, pointing to the little piles and matching them to their crayon names: "Burnt Sienna!" "Carnation Pink!" "Screamin' Green!" "Wild Watermelon!" A week before I left for college Henry died. He was never sick, he never seized or foamed or got tumors — he just came in from playing in the yard one day, curled up on the rug, and passed. He looked very small and very peaceful.

WHERE THE RED FERN GROWS

Skillet Cornbread with Honey Butter

As an East Coaster I wasn't always familiar with the less-sweet Southern iteration of cornbread, but it is lovely, especially paired with this sweet honey butter. If you don't have a cast-iron skillet it is worth investing in one, if only to make a cornbread with edges this sweetly crisp.

Serves 8

4 tablespoons (1/2 stick) unsalted butter, plus extra for the skillet
1/4 cup vegetable shortening
1 1/4 cups fine yellow cornmeal
3/4 cup all-purpose flour
2 tablespoons sugar

2 teaspoons baking powder
1/2 teaspoon baking soda
1 cup buttermilk
1/3 cup whole milk
2 large eggs, beaten
1 or 2 pieces of bacon, ham, or salt pork (optional)

Honey Butter
1/4 cup honey
5 1/3 tablespoons unsalted butter, at room temperature
Kosher salt

Preheat the oven to 375°F.

Melt the butter and shortening in a seasoned cast-iron skillet over medium-high heat. Pour the melted butter and shortening into a dish and rub the remaining grease around in the skillet with a paper towel, making sure to coat the sides. Put the skillet in the oven while you prepare the rest of the ingredients.

Sift together the cornmeal, flour, sugar, baking powder, and baking soda in a large bowl. Add the buttermilk, milk, beaten eggs, and melted butter-shortening mixture. Mix until incorporated, being careful not to overmix; it's okay if the batter is a little bit lumpy.

Remove the skillet from the oven. If you have some bacon, ham, or salt pork, fry it up in the skillet until crispy and remove, leaving the grease in the pan. If not, add a little bit more butter and spread it around the hot pan. Pour the batter into the skillet and bake until a tester inserted into the center comes out clean, about 20 minutes.

While the cornbread is in the oven, make the honey butter. Whip the honey into the softened butter until emulsified. Season with salt to taste. Allow it to set up in the fridge for 5 to 10 minutes before spreading on the hot cornbread.

STREGA NONA
BLACK PEPPER–PARMESAN PASTA

For as long as I can remember, my sisters and I have called my dad Noodle. The name fits him in a number of ways, but it originally stemmed from the fact that no matter what or how much was on the dinner table, my dad never felt that the meal was complete unless it was accompanied by an enormous bowl of pasta. There could be roast beef, potatoes, and a salad, and he would still be in the kitchen fifteen minutes before we sat down, crushing and frying garlic and stirring the pasta pot, the steam blanketing his face with a sheen of tiny, precipitous droplets.

He always made the same thin spaghetti, doused in garlic oil and butter, tossed with loads of crushed black and red pepper, and coated in an avalanche of salty Parmesan. No matter how much we razzed him for it, the bowl was almost always empty by the time we started clearing the table. If it wasn't, the noodles ended up in our lunch the next day, and we munched and slurped them cold, washing down the chewy Parmesan with bright yellow boxes of Yoo-hoo.

Every once in a while my mom would take issue with this ritual, frustrated that she had labored over dinner and still Noodle needed his noodles. One night, my dad had to walk away from the boiling pasta and he asked my mom to stir it. "Make sure you really stir it, Deb," he said. She nodded. "You don't want it to get clumpy," he said, to which my mom turned on her heel and snapped, "OKAY, BIG ANTHONY, I'VE GOT IT." There was a moment of thick silence before they both dissolved into a fit of laughter so powerful that my sisters and I started laughing uncontrollably, too.

"Big Anthony" is the duncelike apprentice to Tomie dePaola's Strega Nona, the grand-motherly witch doctor in his enduringly popular series, who unleashes a landslide of pasta through the town of Calabria when he misuses Strega Nona's magic pasta pot. This book was a mainstay of bedtime reading at the Nicoletti house — my parents read it to my older sister, then to me, then to my younger sister, and my mom still reads it to her nursery school students to this day. De-Paola based his story loosely on a fairy tale recorded by the Brothers Grimm entitled "The Magic Porridge Pot," but the characters of Strega Nona and Big Anthony are all his own. There are now eleven Strega Nona stories, the most recent of which was published in 2011.

Despite being original tales, the Strega Nona books have the folkloric feel of old family stories, passed down through generations. They feel so familiar, in fact, that de-Paola once said that many people come up to him and tell him that their Italian grandparents used to tell them tales of the good witch Strega Nona, as if she had existed for centuries before he created her. This feeling of familiarity is probably one of the reasons the books remain so popular nearly forty years after the first one was published — there is great comfort in tradition. It's this longing for the comfort of tradition that sends me to the pasta pot every time I feel homesick, or lonely, or overwhelmed. I always feel better once the garlic is fried, the noodles are steaming, and the cheese is grated. It's as if my family is all around me, loud and hungry and warm.

STREGA NONA

Black Pepper–Parmesan Pasta
Serves 4

1 pound thin spaghetti
1/4 cup olive oil
4 garlic cloves, smashed
3 teaspoons cracked black pepper
2 tablespoons unsalted butter
2 cups grated good, salty Parmesan
Kosher salt
1 tablespoon crushed red pepper

Bring a large pot of very salty water to a boil over high heat. Add the pasta and cook until al dente (usually around 8 minutes for thin spaghetti, but check the package instructions).

While your pasta is boiling, heat the oil in a very large skillet over medium heat and add the garlic. Cook until the garlic is lightly browned on both sides. Add 2 teaspoons of the black pepper and cook until the pepper is fragrant, another minute or two.

Once the pasta is al dente, reserve 1 cup of the pasta water and then strain out the rest.

Add the butter to the skillet and whisk until it's melted in, then add the reserved 1 cup pasta water and bring it to a boil. Add the pasta to the skillet and sprinkle with 1 1/2 cups of the cheese and toss vigorously with tongs until a creamy sauce forms and coats the pasta, 2 to 3 minutes (you will need a very large skillet — if you don't have one, a large stockpot will also work).

Transfer the contents of the skillet to a large bowl, season with salt to taste, and add the crushed red pepper and the remaining 1 teaspoon black pepper. Garnish with the remaining 1/2 cup Parmesan and serve.

"THE LEGEND OF SLEEPY HOLLOW"

BUCKWHEAT PANCAKES

In the neighborhood where I grew up, there was a family who always went overboard decorating their house for Halloween. Every year it seemed to get more extreme, their lawn decorations veering well past fun and turning sharply into morbid and truly terrifying. The year I was seven, they constructed a headless horseman — a cartoonish stuffed horse mounted by an unsettlingly realistic dummy whose head had been torn off. The stump of a neck was covered in very real-looking blood and gore and the head lay at the feet of the horse, wide-eyed and grimacing — the thought of it haunted me day and night.

In an attempt to ease my terror over the headless horseman, which I had been talking about incessantly since it appeared in mid-September, my dad decided to read me Washington Irving's "The Legend of Sleepy Hollow," thinking that if I heard how silly the real story was, I might not be so scared. It was during this reading, though, that a new terror presented itself to me — one that was much harder for my parents to control.

Early in Irving's description of Ichabod Crane, he tells us that Crane likes to pass his time by terrifying the old Dutch wives "with the alarming fact that the world did absolutely turn round, and that they were half the time topsy-turvy!" Sensing that it was something to be anxious about, I asked my dad what the sentence meant. My older sister, excited that she knew the answer, pulled out her *Simpsons* activity book and pointed to a page showing Otto, the bus driver, with a speech bubble rising from his mouth up into the stars, stating that the earth spun at 1,000 miles per hour.

I stayed in bed for the next three days complaining of being dizzy, gripped with nausea and panic. My mom sent her friend, a child psychiatrist, to ask me what was wrong. When I told her, she asked me questions like, "Okay, so does the spinning bother you because you want things to stay in place and stay the same?" No, lady. I want not to be hurtling around through a giant abyss at top speed! Why is that so hard to understand?

For a long time I thought that this personal, world-altering experience was the only reason that I hated Ichabod Crane as much as I did. When I reread the story in high school, though, I realized that, personal feelings and neuroses aside, Ichabod Crane is simply an unlikable character. He is wimpy, opportunistic, and pathologically self-interested — he is so despicable, in fact, that you barely feel a twinge of sadness over his fate at the story's end.

Nonetheless, I admit that I felt a little bit kindlier toward Ichabod on my second reading for one reason: his insatiable and all-consuming hunger. In the same way that I feel a kindred (if worrisome) connection to Roald Dahl's greedy Augustus Gloop, who nearly meets his death dunking his face into a chocolate pond, and John Kennedy Toole's slothful and gluttonous Ignatius J. Reilly, whose love of hot dogs is practically romantic, I understand Ichabod Crane's ardent love of eating. There is nary a thought that goes through Ichabod's mind that doesn't involve food. When he walks by his neighbor's farm it isn't livestock that he sees, but rather food:

> He pictured to himself every roasting-pig running about with a pudding in his belly, and an apple in his mouth; the pigeons were snugly put to bed in a comfortable pie, and tucked in with a coverlet of crust; geese were swimming in their own gravy; and the ducks pairing cozily in dishes, like snug married couples, with a decent competency of onion sauce. In the porkers he saw carved out the future sleek side of bacon, and juicy relishing ham; not a turkey but he beheld daintily trussed up, with its gizzard under its wing, and, peradventure, a necklace of savory sausages.

Ichabod's love and longing for Katrina Van Tassel is based solely on the fact that her family eats well. His desire for her is so bound up in hunger that he looks at her as if she herself were a meal — "plump as a partridge; ripe and melting and rosy cheeked as one of her father's peaches." It's creepy. But I kind of get it. In one of my favorite autumnal literary passages, Ichabod is walking by a field of buckwheat and imagines its future as pancakes:

As Ichabod jogged slowly on his way, his eye, ever open to every symptom of culinary abundance, ranged with delight over the treasures of jolly autumn. On all sides he beheld vast store of apples; some hanging in oppressive opulence on the trees; some gathered into baskets and barrels for the market; others heaped up in rich piles for the cider-press. Farther on he beheld great fields of Indian corn, with its golden ears peeping from their leafy coverts, and holding out the promise of cakes and hasty pudding; and the yellow pumpkins lying beneath them, turning up their fair round bellies to the sun, and giving ample prospects of the most luxurious of pies; and anon he passed the fragrant buckwheat fields, breathing the odor of the bee-hive, and as he beheld them, soft anticipations stole over his mind of dainty slapjacks, well buttered, and garnished with honey or treacle, by the delicate little dimpled hand of Katrina Van Tassel.

Buckwheat was a staple of the American diet in the eighteenth and nineteenth centuries, but its production took a huge hit in the twentieth with the invention of nitrogen fertilizers. These fertilizers made the cultivation of wheat and maize much easier, and buckwheat lost popularity. I had never eaten a buckwheat anything until I was well into adulthood and working at a restaurant that served buckwheat waffles. The taste and texture were a revelation to me.

"THE LEGEND OF SLEEPY HOLLOW"

Buckwheat Pancakes

This recipe calls for a mix of both white and buckwheat flours. (Despite the name, buckwheat doesn't contain any wheat and is actually related to rhubarb, sorrel, and knotweed, so if you are gluten intolerant, feel free to sub out the white flour and use all buckwheat; the pancakes may be a little denser but they will still be delicious.) Yogurt lightens the buckwheat's denseness, and brown butter brings out its nutty earthiness. These pancakes are great served with honey or maple syrup, butter and jelly, peanut butter and bananas, or, for a more savory breakfast, crème fraîche and smoked salmon (I've tried them with all of these toppings, for research purposes, of course).

Makes 8 to 10 pancakes

5 tablespoons unsalted butter
2 large eggs, separated
2 tablespoons sugar
1 cup plain full-fat Greek yogurt
1/4 cup water
1 teaspoon pure vanilla extract
3/4 cup buckwheat flour
1/2 cup all-purpose flour
4 teaspoons baking soda
1/2 teaspoon kosher salt
Favorite toppings (see headnote), for serving

Brown 3 tablespoons of the butter and set it aside to cool.

Place the egg yolks in a large bowl. Add the sugar and whisk until the yolks are a creamy light yellow. Add the yogurt, water, vanilla, and browned butter and whisk until combined.

In a separate bowl, whisk together both flours, the baking soda, and the salt. Whisk the dry ingredients into the wet mixture.

In a medium bowl, whisk the egg whites until they reach stiff peaks. (Alternatively, you can do this part in an electric mixer with a whisk attachment.) Gently fold the stiff whites into the batter until they are fully incorporated.

Preheat the oven to 150°F (for keeping the finished pancakes warm while the others cook).

Melt the remaining 2 tablespoons butter in a medium skillet (preferably cast-iron) over medium heat and scoop about 1/4 cup batter into the pan. Cook until bubbles begin to form all over the pancake, about 3 minutes, flip, and cook until the bottom is crisp and brown, about 3 minutes more. Repeat with the remaining batter, transferring the finished pancakes to the warm oven until all are done. Serve with your favorite toppings.

■ ■ ■ ■

PART 2
ADOLESCENCE &
COLLEGE YEARS

■ ■ ■ ■

To Kill a Mockingbird
BISCUITS WITH MOLASSES BUTTER

The year I was nine my best friends Christie and Meg and I discovered a haunted house in the woods at the edge of Christie's neighborhood. I'm not sure exactly what made us think that it was haunted, other than the fact that it was condemned and falling apart. The front porch sagged in like a sinkhole and in the upstairs rooms lacy, yellowed curtains blew from breezes let in through a smashed window. It was so unlike any of the other houses in the neighborhood, which were all sunny and welcoming with well-groomed yards, that we assumed something terrible must have happened there.

We visited the house almost every day after school, watching it through binoculars from behind a tree to see if we could spot a ghost moving around behind the windows and, when we were feeling really brave, leaving notes on the front porch written in invisible ink. Every day when I got home, my dad would ruffle my mushroom cut and say, "Hey, Scout, did you find Boo Radley today?"

I finally found out what he meant when he left his worn-out copy of Harper Lee's classic novel, *To Kill a Mockingbird,* on my bedside table that year. I may have been slightly too young to understand exactly what was going on in the book, but I loved it regardless. The connection that I felt to Scout, with her mischievous, rough-and-tumble exterior and sensitive interior, remains one of the most intense I've ever had. I fell so deeply in love with the empathetic and fiercely moral Jem that I scribbled his name in my notebook on more than one occasion, wishing that he was as real as I felt he was.

Along with the characters, I fell in love with Southern food, too — or at least with the *idea* of it. There were cracklin' bread and scuppernongs, dewberry tarts, peach pickles, hickory nuts, cherry wine, butter beans, and a Lane cake "loaded with shinny" — I barely knew what any of it was, but I knew it all *sounded* better than anything I ate at home. When I was growing up on the East Coast, the closest I got to a real biscuit was a McDonald's bacon, egg, and cheese biscuit, a rare family road-trip treat.

As much as I loved those sandwiches, it never occurred to me that I might be missing out in the biscuit department until I read *To Kill a Mockingbird* and realized that in the South, biscuits weren't just a breakfast treat, they were an every-meal staple. The residents of Maycomb sit on the lawn of the courthouse and eat biscuits with syrup and warm milk, they sop up their collard juice with them, and they spread them with molasses and butter. When Jem and Scout are hungry before dinner, their cook, Calpurnia, sends them outside with a hot biscuit slathered in butter to tide them over. Biscuits are so ubiquitous, in fact, that at one point Calpurnia even uses cold ones to shine Scout's patent-leather shoes.

After reading the book, I pestered my mom to make at least one of the fifty-two foods I had read about (yes, I counted). The best were biscuits made from Bisquick mix, which was more than good enough for me. I learned to make them myself and ate them as often as I was allowed. Besides McDonald's, this was truly the only biscuit I knew until about eight years ago, when Southern food exploded in popularity in Brooklyn. Suddenly it seemed as if every restaurant was serving Southern-style comfort food, claiming that their fried chicken, shrimp and grits, and pulled pork were the best. The true test of which was the best, for me, was easy — it was all about the biscuit.

In early 2010 I started working as a baker at one of these Southern comfort restaurants in Brooklyn, and the reality of what it meant to serve biscuits with almost every meal hit home. All day long we made biscuits, fifty at a time. It was endless. There always had to be a backup of frozen butter cut into flour in huge bus-tubs, ready to be mixed with buttermilk at a moment's notice. Running out of biscuits was simply not an option.

Maybe I'm still making up for lost time on my biscuit consumption, but despite having baked literally thousands of biscuits in the past four years and eaten well into the hundreds, I am still not sick of them, and they are still one of my favorite things to bake. Looking for something to do with our excess lard every week at the Meat Hook, the butcher shop where I now work in Brooklyn, I started experimenting with using it in a biscuit mix and it has quickly become my favorite way to make them. The lard has a savory, salty quality, and because it melts more slowly than butter, the biscuits are fluffier and airier than any I have ever eaten. They're especially delicious with sweet and salty molasses butter.

TO KILL A MOCKINGBIRD

Biscuits with Molasses Butter

You can get leaf lard from your butcher. (Do not buy the hydrogenated lard on supermarket shelves.) If you are a vegetarian, feel free to leave out the lard and use all butter.

Makes 10 to 12 (3-inch) biscuits

1 cup pastry flour
2 tablespoons baking powder
1 1/2 teaspoons kosher salt
1 teaspoon baking soda
8 tablespoons (1 stick) unsalted butter
1/2 cup (4 ounces) rendered leaf lard

3 cups all-purpose flour
1 1/4 to 1 1/2 cups buttermilk
1 egg
1 tablespoon cream
Molasses Butter (recipe follows)

In a mixing bowl, whisk together the pastry flour, baking powder, salt, and baking soda. Cut the butter and leaf lard into cubes (roughly 1 inch, don't stress about it) and toss them in the flour mixture. Put the bowl in the freezer until the butter and leaf lard are completely frozen, about an hour.

Once the fats are frozen and the dry ingredients are icy cold, transfer the mixture to a food processor and pulse until pea-sized chunks of fat are distributed throughout the flour. Transfer the mixture to a large bowl and add the all-purpose flour. Toss until the butter and lard are spread evenly throughout.

Add 1 1/4 cups of the buttermilk and mix gently. Test to see if the dough holds together when you squeeze it. If it doesn't, add the remaining 1/4 cup buttermilk, tablespoon by tablespoon, until it does.

Line a baking sheet with parchment paper or a silicone baking mat. Bring the dough together on a lightly floured surface and roll to 3/4 inch thick. Cut the dough into 3-inch rounds with a circle cutter and place the biscuits on the lined baking sheet. You can reroll once with the leftover scraps of dough, but that batch won't be quite as fluffy.

Place the biscuits in the freezer while you preheat the oven to 400°F.

Beat the egg and cream together and brush the tops of the cold biscuits with the egg wash. Bake until golden brown, 20 to 25 minutes. Serve warm with molasses butter.

Note: You can freeze the formed, unbaked biscuits for a quick treat another day. Once they have frozen solid on the baking sheet, transfer them to a zip-top plastic bag. Egg-wash them right before you bake them and put them into the oven still frozen. They will need an additional 5 or 10 minutes of baking time.

Molasses Butter
Makes about 3/4 cup

8 tablespoons (1 stick) unsalted butter, at
    room temperature
2 tablespoons light brown sugar
Generous pinch of flaky sea salt (such as

Maldon)
1/4 cup unsulphured molasses

In the bowl of an electric mixer fitted with a paddle attachment, beat together the butter, brown sugar, and sea salt until light and fluffy. Add the molasses and continue to beat until incorporated throughout. Spread on biscuits or transfer to a ramekin, cover, and refrigerate for up to 1 week.

Lord of the Flies
PORCHETTA DI TESTA

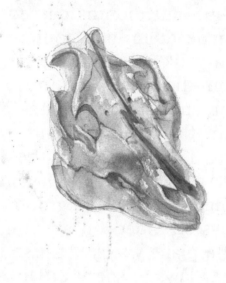

When I was very young — probably seven — the 1963 film version of *Lord of the Flies* was on television one night. It was Christmastime and I was sitting next to my mom and dad on the couch when my dad, flipping through the channels, stumbled across it and stopped. For the next three hours I sat still as stone, *terrified* by what I was watching, but too shy to tell my parents.

As I lay in bed that night trying to sleep, the image of the fly-covered pig's head, a stake stuck into its neck, kept going through my tiny stressed-out brain. It's not as if I had never seen a pig's head before. I saw them often at my grandfather's butcher shop, but they were hairless and pale pink, eyes half-shut and mouths curved up in a way that made them look content — they were nothing like that hairy, bulgy-eyed monster from the movie. For the remainder of that night, and for a few nights following, I slept on the floor of my parents' room.

Years later I was assigned the novel in school and was rattled all over again by William Golding's account of a group of young English boys stranded on an uninhabited island after a plane wreck. At first, the boys adhere to the laws of social order they have been raised with — calling meetings, electing leaders, dividing labor — but as the novel progresses, this order quickly crumbles and the reader watches, realizing along with Ralph that "the world, that understandable and lawful world, was slipping away." Golding strands this specific age group — boys between six and twelve years old — because they are particularly susceptible to shedding societal constraints. In showing us how quickly this mini society plunges into chaos, he challenges the notion that humans are inherently civilized.

When the boys first land on the island, their proper English manners and habits are still deeply ingrained. Faced with the prospect of having to kill a pig because everyone is hungry, Jack is unable to follow through, "because of the enormity of the knife descending and cutting into living flesh; because of the unbearable blood." Only two chapters later, however, Jack slits a pig's throat and proudly comes back to the camp with the "knowledge that they had outwitted a living thing, imposed their will upon it, taken away its life like a long satisfying drink."

When the "littluns" start to worry that there is a beast lurking around the island, panic spreads throughout the camp and Jack decides to take the head of the pig they killed and present it as an offering to appease the beast. The pig's head, which they call the Lord of the Flies, comes to represent chaos and disorder, savagery and the instinctual brutality of human nature (I learned only recently that the literal translation of Beelzebub is "lord of the flies"). The image is so powerful, both in film and in writing, that even now, having de-faced countless pigs' heads at the Meat Hook, I still think about *Lord of the Flies* every time I do it.

The truth is, pigs' heads are absolutely delicious if you are willing to take the time to prepare them the right way. It seems intimidating, but it's much easier than you would expect.

LORD OF THE FLIES

Porchetta di Testa

Most local butcher shops have pigs' heads on hand, and if not, they will usually be happy to special-order one for you. For this recipe, ask your butcher to take the meat off the head in one piece and clean it of all the glands. Then all that's left to do is spice it, tie it up as you would a roast, and cook it. It goes great over a bed of lentils, potatoes, or stewed greens.

Serves 8 to 10

Meat of 1 pig's head, all in one piece, including ears and tongue, cleaned of all glands (about 7 pounds of meat)
4 tablespoons kosher salt
1 tablespoon plus 1 teaspoon fennel seeds, toasted

2 1/4 teaspoons freshly ground black pepper
1 1/2 teaspoons crushed red pepper
Finely chopped leaves of 2 rosemary sprigs
Finely chopped leaves of 2 thyme sprigs
15 garlic cloves, put through a garlic press
Zest of 2 lemons plus 1 tablespoon lemon juice
1 teaspoon plus 2 tablespoons olive oil, divided

First, you're going to clean the meat up a bit, which includes shaving the outside meat with a razor if there is any hair (come on, it's fun!). Also make sure that there are no glands, and that the hard collagen from the nostrils and ear canals are cut out — your butcher should have done this for you, but it doesn't hurt to check. Now, in a large mortar, combine 2 tablespoons of the salt and the rest of the ingredients except the 2 tablespoons oil and mash them up with a pestle until a nice paste forms.

Spread the face meat in front of you, skin-side down. Tuck the ears backward, up through the eyeholes, so that the holes are covered, and flatten them out. Rub the seasoning paste all over the meat. Lay the tongue flat along the inside of the snout and rub it with any remaining seasoning paste.

Starting with the jowl on one side, roll up

the meat like a jelly roll. Tie the cylinder tightly with twine as you would a roast, set it in a roasting pan on a roasting rack, and place it in the refrigerator, uncovered, to cure overnight. The next day, take the roast out and let it sit at room temperature for 1 1/2 hours.

Preheat the oven to 450°F.

Rub the outside of the roast with the remaining 2 tablespoons salt and roast for 20 minutes.

Lower the heat to 250°F, cover the roasting pan with aluminum foil, and cook for an additional 2 1/2 hours. Remove the foil and brush the skin with the remaining 2 tablespoons olive oil. Bump up the heat to 325°F and continue to roast for 30 minutes. (This should get the skin crispy.) The roast should reach an internal temperature of 140°F.

Remove the roast from the oven and allow it to rest for 20 minutes before slicing crosswise and serving.

THE CATCHER IN THE RYE
MALTED MILK ICE CREAM

I know I'm not alone in saying that middle school, particularly eighth grade, was absolute hell. It was so bad, in fact, that even now I tend to distrust anyone who looks back fondly on the ages eleven to fourteen. It was in eighth grade, after a particularly gut-wrenching day during which I was unceremoniously dumped by all of my girlfriends, that my English teacher, Mr. Mitchell, gave me a copy of *The Catcher in the Rye*.

I had just eaten lunch in the nurse's office on a trundle bed covered in white paper, and I arrived to his class blotchy-faced and glassy-eyed, looking like a crazed and frizzy Catholic schoolgirl zombie — the "Thriller" version of "Baby One More Time." Oh, did I not mention? To add insult to injury, I was wearing a Britney Spears costume that day — it was Halloween 1999, okay? I'm sure that Mr. Mitchell, who had a daughter of his own and who had been doing battle in the trenches of middle school for at least twenty years, was familiar with this kind of scene. After class, he listened to me blubber with a kind of quiet empathy that still makes my throat swell to think about, and he pressed a copy of Salinger's book into my hands.

The novel was exactly what I needed at the time — a testament to the fact that adolescence is agonizing, confusing, lonely. I stayed obsessed with it, and with Holden, all through high school, revisiting it for comfort whenever I was feeling particularly overwhelmed with being a teenager. I wore a maroon T-shirt on which I'd ironed on felt letters that said "I am Holden Caulfield." As a final English project freshman year, I created a *Catcher in the Rye* soundtrack, which I called "Hearing Holden," filled with torturously sad songs by the Smiths and Azure Ray. (If you're wondering if I had more fun in high school than I did in middle school, the answer is no, I didn't.)

The older I got, though, the less Salinger's writing sang to me, and by college I had put my twice-yearly *Catcher in the Rye* reading habit to rest. The other night, I reread it for the first time in eight years, and to my surprise I found it nearly unbearable. This could be due, in part, to the simple fact that I grew up — that I'm no longer as melancholy or bitter or determined to be misunderstood as I was when *The Catcher in the Rye* first pulled me from despair as a thirteen-year-old. It could also be due to the fact that I've learned too much about J. D. Salinger's personal life in the years since his death to read his fiction as purely fiction ever again.

When he passed away in 2010, a media frenzy broke loose, rehashing every lurid detail of the intensely private Salinger's life and adding previously unknown biographical tidbits — none of them particularly flattering. It was during this time that I learned about his tumultuous relationships with young girls, his religious practices, his work habits, his sexual dysfunction, his paranoia. I learned, too, about his eating habits, which included a strict organic and macrobiotic diet.

According to *At Home in the World,* the memoir written by his famously spurned lover, Joyce Maynard, Salinger avoided cooking any of his food, if possible, believing that "cooking food robs it of all of its natural nutrients"; when he did cook it, he was very specific about his methods and his cooking oils. He shunned pasteurized dairy products, "refined foods like sugar and white flour — even whole wheat flour, honey, and maple syrup." In Raychel Haugrud Reiff's 2008 biography of Salinger, she revealed that for breakfast he and Maynard would eat "whole grain bread and frozen peas, and for dinner bread, steamed fiddlehead ferns, apple slices, and sometimes popcorn. If they had meat, it was barely cooked organic ground lamb." Maynard also claims that after going out to eat pizza with his son, Salinger would make himself vomit in order to "rid his body of impure food."

I'm not particularly interested in Salinger's food issues, but in relation to his fiction they fascinate me, because his stories are full of eating-disordered characters. There is Franny, of *Franny and Zooey,* who refuses to eat while on her dinner date with Lane Coutell, not even picking at the chicken sandwich or sipping her glass of milk as her irritated date stabs at his frog legs and escargot. She is sickly and shivering, and once the waiter takes away her untouched food she falls into a faint on her way to the restroom. Once home, she argues with her mother about her refusal to eat.

In "A Perfect Day for Bananafish," Seymour Glass and a little girl named Sybil discuss how they both like to chew on candle wax. Seymour then launches into a story about his invented bananafish, who "lead a very tragic life." "They swim into a hole," he tells her, "where there's a lot of bananas. They're very ordinary-looking fish when they swim *in.* But once they get in, they behave like pigs," he says, gorging themselves on so many bananas that they are sadly unable to get back out of the hole. After this strange, make-believe story about the dangers of overeating, Seymour goes back to his hotel room and shoots himself in the head.

Then, of course, there is Holden Caulfield, who professes to be "a very light eater" — unusual for a sixteen-year-old boy.

He usually has just orange juice for breakfast, which is why he's "so damn skinny." He alludes to the fact that at one point he was put on a special diet "where you eat a lot of starches and crap, to gain weight and all," but he "didn't ever do it." Holden then tells us his usual order when he's out somewhere, which is one of my favorite literary meals of all: "a Swiss cheese sandwich and a malted milk." "It isn't much," he says, "but you get quite a lot of vitamins in the malted milk. H. V. Caulfield. Holden Vitamin Caulfield."

It's a meal packed with the pasteurized dairy, refined sugars, and white flour that Salinger so feared, but the concern for health is still quietly there. Malted milk powder is a mixture of barley malt, wheat flour, and evaporated milk, and was originally sold as a health food. Malt sugars are easily digestible, so it was thought that malt powder would be easy on the stomachs of infants and the very ill. Because of its delicious, toasty, caramelized flavors, it makes a dreamy companion for ice cream, and it became a soda fountain staple for Holden Caulfield's generation.

Malted Milk Ice Cream

Holden's malted milk could simply be malt powder stirred into a glass of milk, but I like to imagine that it's a malted milkshake. Here, the choice is yours: use this malted milk ice cream to make a shake, or just eat it on its own.

Makes about 1 quart

1 1/2 cups whole milk
1 1/2 cups heavy cream
2 vanilla beans, seeds scraped out and pods reserved
1/3 cup malt powder
3 large egg yolks
1/2 cup sugar
3/4 teaspoon kosher salt
1/2 cup chocolate malted milk candies (such as Whoppers), crushed slightly

Prepare an ice bath by filling the sink or a very large bowl with ice cubes and cold water. Place a large metal or glass bowl over the ice bath and a fine-mesh strainer over the bowl.

In a large, heavy-bottomed pot, whisk together the milk, cream, and vanilla seeds and pods over medium heat until you see small bubbles start to form around the edge of the pot and steam rising from the surface of the liquid. Whisk in the malt powder and remove the pot from the heat.

In a large bowl, whisk together the egg yolks, sugar, and salt until pale yellow. Whisking constantly, very slowly pour in the hot milk mixture in a steady stream until it is fully incorporated.

Pour this mixture back into the pot and whisk constantly over medium-low heat until it reaches 170°F on a candy thermometer, about 10 minutes. Pour it through the strainer into the bowl set over the ice bath and whisk until it cools to room temperature. Cover the bowl and transfer it to the refrigerator to chill for at least 8 hours.

Churn the chilled base in an ice cream maker according to the manufacturer's directions. When the ice cream has set, add the crushed malted milk candies and process in the ice cream maker until they are incorporated throughout, about 30 more seconds of spinning.

Let the ice cream set up in the freezer for about an hour before serving.

THE BELL JAR
CRAB-STUFFED AVOCADOS

Sylvia Plath holds a special place in my heart, because her childhood home was directly across the street from the house I grew up in. As a child, I spent many long hours staring at the window I imagined was her bedroom. It seemed incredible to me that such a simple box of a house, with its white clapboard siding and shiny black shutters, could have contained a mind so enormous.

I didn't know about Plath until I was in

fourth grade, when my mom casually told me that a very famous writer named Sylvia Plath had grown up in the house across the street. At the time, I was up to my ears in the Redwall and Golden Compass series, filled with dreams of someday becoming a writer. I simply could not believe that a very famous *female* writer had grown up across the street and my mom had never thought to tell me about it.

This was, of course, pre-Google, a world in which you did not have access to every intimate detail of a person's life at the click of a button. So that afternoon I rode my bike to the library. I asked the librarian where I could find Sylvia Plath's books, and she looked at me in a concerned way but led me to the stacks. I spent hours on the floor of the library that day, trying to make sense of just one line of Plath's poetry, but I left with only a vague sense of dread that I would never be happy again once I turned ten.

I spent the next decade staring out the window at the white house across the street and attempting to read Plath's poetry, but it wasn't until my junior year of high school, when my favorite English teacher gave me *The Bell Jar,* that I found Plath accessible for the first time. In this semiautobiographical novel, which Plath published under the pen name Victoria Lucas in 1963, a young woman named Esther Greenwood travels to New York City for a summer internship at *Ladies' Day* magazine.

Esther ultimately has to leave New York after suffering a mental breakdown, and the novel follows her descent into mental illness as she attempts suicide on multiple occasions, is put in an asylum, and receives treatment from various doctors (including electroshock therapy and insulin injections). Plath eases the reader into Esther's degeneration with such subtlety that it takes a moment to realize that Esther has truly and completely lost her mind. The novel is bleak, there is no denying it, but I found Esther so likable (though I've heard others say different) and her voice so original that I kept reading it just to root for her.

When Esther first arrives in New York, before everything begins to fall apart for her, she goes to a luncheon for *Ladies' Day.* It was this passage, about Esther's relationship with food, that made me fall for her right away — I love a girl who isn't shy about pigging out at an elegant affair. Surrounded by young women too timid and dainty to eat, Esther begins to load up her plate, emboldened by her belief that "if you do something incorrect at a table with a certain arrogance," and act as if you know exactly what you are doing, "nobody will think you are bad-mannered or poorly brought up. They will think you are original and very witty."

With this philosophy in her back pocket, Esther approaches the food at the luncheon fearlessly, piling caviar on thin slices of chicken before moving on to "tackle the avocado and crabmeat salad." Avocados, Esther explains, are her favorite fruit. Every Sunday, her grandfather would bring her "an avocado pear hidden at the bottom of his briefcase under six soiled shirts and the Sunday comics." He taught her how to eat avocados by filling their hollows with a special garnet sauce he made from grape jelly and French dressing. Esther eats the avocado and crabmeat and feels "homesick for that sauce. The crabmeat tasted bland in comparison."

Almost immediately after the luncheon Esther and all the other girls fall violently ill with food poisoning. In the haze of her illness, Esther envisions "avocado pear after avocado pear being stuffed with crabmeat and mayonnaise and photographed under brilliant lights." She sees "the delicate, pink-mottled claw meat poking seductively through its blanket of mayonnaise and the bland yellow pear cup with its rim of alligator-green cradling the whole mess."

There is something wonderfully kitschy about a crabmeat-stuffed avocado, but I can't imagine that what Esther ate that day would appeal to most of us now (I'm thinking lots and lots of mayonnaise). This crab salad is bright and fresh, loaded with herbs and fresh lemon juice — and no mayonnaise in sight.

THE BELL JAR

Crab-Stuffed Avocados
Makes 4 stuffed avocado halves

1 pound fresh crabmeat, picked over
Juice of 1 lemon (about 1/4 cup)
3 tablespoons olive oil
2 teaspoons finely chopped fresh parsley
2 teaspoons finely chopped fresh dill
2 teaspoons finely chopped fresh cilantro
Kosher salt
Freshly ground black pepper
2 ripe avocados, halved and pitted

Toss together the crabmeat, lemon juice, olive oil, and herbs in a large glass bowl and season with salt and pepper to taste. Divide the salad evenly among the four avocado halves and serve.

REBECCA
BLOOD ORANGE MARMALADE

When I was fifteen, I was dumped by my first love, a boy nearly three years my senior, while eating a baked potato covered in neon-orange cheese sauce in the school cafeteria. Thirteen years later I still remember everything about that day — what I wore (a yellow T-shirt that said "Blondes

Have More Fun") and who I talked to, what we read in English class (*Romeo and Juliet*) and how, after school, I got sick in a neon-orange cheese sauce kind of way from the physical blow of how desperately sad I felt. A heady mixture of hula-hooping hormones and genuine hurt knocked me off my feet so intensely that my mom swears even now that my eyes changed color that day, in the same way that people's hair can turn white from shock.

There was, of course, another girl — an ex-girlfriend — older and cooler and infinitely more beautiful than the bony elbows and caterpillar-thick eyebrows I saw when I looked in the mirror. For weeks I walked around in a fog, jealousy and betrayal roiling and churning in my gut like a disease, grades slipping and friends growing tired of me. One day I walked into my bedroom after school to find a book sitting on my pillow, lavender and blue with loopy pink cursive scrawled across it: *Rebecca.* My mom had placed it on my bed in an attempt to distract me from my despair, and upon seeing it I suddenly realized, astonished, that I hadn't picked up a book in weeks. It was the longest I'd gone without reading since I started at age six. I was mortified at how far away I had gotten from myself, and

I tore into the book as if it was the only hope I had of remembering who I had once been.

Rebecca is almost always described as a gothic romance novel. Year after year around Valentine's Day it pops up on various Internet lists compiling the most romantic literature of all time. Next to snapshots of its various vampy, supermarket-paperback covers, there is always a blurb about the novel's dashing and stoic Maxim de Winter, whose dark secrets and cold demeanor only serve to make him more compelling. Maybe it's because I first read *Rebecca* with a broken heart, but to me this book is not at all romantic. To me, *Rebecca* is a story about jealousy, revenge, rage, identity, and how completely a person can be swallowed by a love that is neither equal nor returned. The narrator, a meek girl in her early twenties, goes unnamed throughout the entire novel, which I found particularly poignant and disturbing during my own heartsick identity crisis.

Daphne du Maurier always said that *Rebecca* was a study in jealousy, but she rarely mentioned that the inspiration for the novel stemmed from events in her own life. Just as our unnamed narrator struggles with the feeling that she will never be equal to her husband's mysteriously deceased first wife, Rebecca, so too did du Maurier struggle with feelings of jealousy and inadequacy in her own marriage. Du Maurier's husband, Tommy Browning, had been engaged to a woman named Jan Ricardo before he married du Maurier in 1932. Ricardo was a dark and glamorous figure, a woman who signed her elegantly written letters to Browning with an intricately curling R, much like du Maurier's own Rebecca de Winter, whose name "stood out black and strong, the tall and sloping R dwarfing the other letters."

Rebecca is brimming with mouthwatering food. The breakfasts at Manderley (the de Winter estate) are awe-inspiring, particularly to our narrator, who is used to so much less. There are scrambled eggs and bacon, fish, boiled eggs, porridge, and ham. There is an entire table of condiments for the toast and scones — jam, marmalade, and honey — as well as dessert dishes and mountains of fresh fruit. The foods are simple and comforting, but the sheer amount leaves the narrator wondering, after Maxim takes only a small piece of fish from this bounty, what happens to all the food that goes untouched.

These food scenes are not just space fillers. What the characters eat — and how they order it, eat it (or don't eat it), and think about it — speaks volumes about who they are and what their positions are. At the beginning of the novel we learn exactly what type of person Mrs. Van Hopper is when we see her eat ravioli with her "fat, bejeweled fingers . . . her eyes darting suspiciously from her plate to mine for fear I should have made the better choice." We learn about the narrator's social position via food as well, when the waiter who "had long sensed my position as inferior and subservient to [Mrs. Van Hopper's], had placed before me a plate of ham and tongue that somebody had sent back to the cold buffet half an hour before as badly carved."

To me, the most poignant, character-exposing food scene in the novel comes at the end of the narrator's trip to Monte Carlo, when Maxim de Winter proposes marriage over toast and marmalade. Without even a hello, Maxim barks at the waiter, "Bring me coffee, a boiled egg, toast, marmalade, and a tangerine," all the while filing his nails with an emery board that was stashed in his pocket. The narrator misinterprets his vague invitation to come back with him to Manderley, thinking that perhaps he needs a new servant. He snaps at her, saying, "I'm asking you to marry me, you little fool." In the confusion that follows, the narrator watches a fly settle on the marmalade, which Maxim brushes away from the jam impatiently before digging into it to spread thickly on his toast. This has to be the least romantic proposal in the history of literature, maybe in the history of history, and it is made infinitely more grotesque by Maxim's food etiquette.

I was a young, brokenhearted girl, and this scene screamed at me. I had been wondering endlessly in those weeks what warning signs I had missed, overanalyzing every past conversation and trying to recall body language in the hopes that I could find the one shining clue that I had overlooked, the thing that should have told me to run, the fly in the marmalade. It is true what our unnamed narrator says, that first love "is a fever, and a burden, too, whatever the poets may say." Thankfully, for both me and our narrator, "it cannot happen twice, that fever of first love." I have been loved and hurt a thousand times since, but none stung so much as the first.

Blood Orange Marmalade

I hope the fly hasn't put you off the idea of marmalade. This recipe is made with blood oranges, but if they aren't in season you can easily make it with any kind of orange available.

Makes about 2 cups

3 blood oranges
4 cups water
2 cups sugar
2 1/2 tablespoons fresh lemon juice
1 tablespoon grated fresh lemon zest

Using a small, sharp knife, cut the rind and pith away from the blood oranges. Discard the pith and slice the rind into 1/8-inch-thick strips. Slice the peeled oranges into thin rounds and place them, along with the peel strips, in a heavy-bottomed pot. Cover with the water and allow them to sit at room temperature overnight, or at least 8 hours, to help the peels begin to soften.

After the peels have soaked, place the pot on the stove and bring the mixture to a boil over medium-high heat, stirring occasionally. Reduce the heat to medium and simmer until the peels have softened and the liquid has reduced significantly, about 1 1/2 hours.

Stir in the sugar, whisking to incorporate, and continue to cook until the mixture reaches 220°F. (If you don't have a candy or deep-fry thermometer, place a plate in the refrigerator before you start this process to get it thoroughly chilled. Once you think the jam is thick enough, test it by spooning a small amount onto the chilled plate and waiting about 5 minutes. If the marmalade firms up and forms a skin, it's ready; if not, keep boiling.)

Once the marmalade reaches temperature, stir in the lemon juice and zest and pour the mixture into two sterilized 1-cup canning jars. Process them according to the canning jar instructions, or store the marmalade in unprocessed jars in the refrigerator for up to 2 months.

Les Misérables

BLACK RYE BREAD

When people talk about *Les Misérables,* it's rare that they're referring to Victor Hugo's 1862 novel. Embarrassingly enough, until I was fifteen, I didn't know that it was a book at all. I did, however, know a good bit about the musical from Julia, one of my childhood best friends, because her parents took her to New York City every year to see it.

Julia was the ultimate girly-girl, and her bedroom was absolutely fascinating to me — all floral country bedding and lacy bed skirts. It was nothing like the bedroom I shared with my sisters, my corner of which was covered in reproductions of antique baseball cards that I had bought at Bop City Comics and stuck to the wall with my older sister's orthodontic wax. The centerpiece of Julia's bedroom was her prized possession: a dome-shaped glass music box filled with fiber-optic flowers that spit light like some kind of deep-sea amoeba and swayed to "Castle on a Cloud" when she turned the dome's big iron crank. I hated that thing and wanted it, *needed* it, in equal measure. It tortured me.

Years later, my aunt gave me a beautiful copy of *Les Misérables* as a fifteenth birthday gift, and I learned for the first time that it wasn't just a musical, but an enormous and very serious-looking book — one that looked nothing like the inspiration for Julia's dome of flowers or the precious song that emanated from it. I tore through it in a week and a half, staying up late and neglecting my freshman-year assigned reading to find out whom Marius would end up with. I loved Jean Valjean through all of his transformations and missteps, going so far as to scribble his name inside a heart in the bathroom stall at school where every girl wrote the initials of her crush in ragged ballpoint pen. I feel very raw admitting this, even now.

Despite my love of the book, I still have yet to see the musical, or the film version either. It could be that these adaptations will always be too much associated with Julia's girliness, or that in general I despise musicals (which could also be Julia's doing), but I just can't get myself excited about either rendition. The constant loop of the trailers on TV and the barrage of posters in every subway did fill me with the desire to read the book again, though — a decision that immediately thwarted my New Year's resolution to eat less bread in 2013.

Any discussion about food in *Les Misérables* (or really any discussion about *Les Misérables* at all) would be incomplete without the mention of bread. The entire plot of the novel is driven by Jean Valjean's nineteen-year imprisonment for stealing a loaf of bread to feed his starving family. The French Revolution is always quietly (and sometimes not so quietly) present in the novel, which mostly takes place in 1815, just fifteen years after Marie Antoinette reportedly declared "Let them eat cake" upon hearing that the peasants had no bread to eat. Throughout the novel, people's stations and the direness of their situations are often described in relation to whether or not they have bread or, more often, what kind of bread they do have.

When we first meet Jean Valjean he has just been released from prison, and he is wandering through Digne starving after being turned away from every inn and household for being an ex-prisoner. Finally, he is sent to Bishop Myriel's house, where he is given one of my favorite literary meals, "a piece of mutton, figs, a fresh cheese, and a loaf of rye bread," as well as a bottle of old Mauves wine. The meal is beautiful in its simplicity, and especially satisfying after reading pages and pages describing Valjean's desperate hunger.

Black rye bread was prevalent throughout France at the time *Les Misérables* was written. It was a staple for lower- and middle-class people alike, and was one of the main foods provided in prisons like the one Valjean lived in for nineteen years. This black rye is nothing like what Valjean would have eaten in prison — it is sweet and bitter and complex and incredibly delicious.

Black Rye Bread

This bread would be great topped with cream cheese and lox, or honey and butter, or almond butter — or, of course, a piece of mutton, figs, and a fresh cheese.

Makes 1 loaf

1 1/3 cups warm water (110°F)
2 1/4 teaspoons active dry yeast (1 packet)
1 teaspoon dark brown sugar
2 tablespoons unsweetened cocoa powder
2 tablespoons instant espresso powder
1/4 cup unsulphured molasses
3 tablespoons unsalted butter
2 tablespoons caraway seeds, plus more for
   topping
2 teaspoons fine sea salt
3 1/4 cups bread flour
1 1/3 cups rye flour
Olive oil, for brushing
Flaky sea salt (such as Maldon), for sprinkling on top

Combine the warm water, yeast, and brown sugar in the bowl of an electric mixer fitted with a dough hook attachment, but don't turn on the mixer. Within about 10 minutes the yeast should be foamy — if it isn't, toss it and start again (you had a dud yeast packet).

Meanwhile, combine the cocoa powder, espresso powder, molasses, butter, caraway seeds, and salt in a small saucepan and stir constantly over medium heat until the butter is melted and the ingredients are well combined. Remove the molasses mixture from the heat and let it sit for a minute so that it is not scorching hot, and add it to the active yeast mixture in the mixer bowl.

In a separate bowl combine the flours and, with the mixer on medium, slowly add the flours to the molasses-yeast mixture. Once everything comes together, knead the dough until it is pulling away from the sides of the bowl and hugging the dough hook, about 5 minutes. The dough should spring back when you poke your thumb into it. If it is too dry, add more water; if it is too wet, add more bread flour, until you get the desired consistency. Shape the dough into a ball and place it, seam-side down, in an oiled bowl. Cover loosely with a towel and let it rise in a warm place for 2 hours.

After 2 hours, gently punch down the risen dough and turn it out onto a floured work surface. Shape the dough into your desired shape, place it in a Dutch oven (or any heavy-bottomed, oven-safe dish or pot with a lid), and allow it to rise until doubled in size, another 1 or 2 hours.

Preheat the oven to 425°F.

Brush the bread with olive oil and sprinkle it with caraway seeds and flaky sea salt. When the oven is up to temperature, put the lid on the Dutch oven and bake for 20 minutes. After 20 minutes remove the lid and turn the heat down to 350°F. Continue baking until the bread sounds hollow when it is tapped, another 20 to 25 minutes. Cool on a wire rack before slicing.

GREAT EXPECTATIONS
PORK PIE

Pity the pork pie in *Great Expectations* — it is always upstaged by Miss Havisham's rotten "bride-cake." It's hard to talk about any food other than Miss Havisham's vermininfested wedding cake when *Great Expectations* is mentioned, and I am certainly guilty of this habit. I have been trying to re-create that cake in all of its decrepit glory ever since I read the book in high school and became completely obsessed with Miss Havisham. As far as driving the plot of the novel, though, that bride-cake doesn't do half as much as the pilfered pork pie. I think it's high time that we give it its due.

When we first meet Pip, he is only six years old, sitting in a church graveyard surveying the graves of his father, mother, and five siblings, who "gave up trying to get a living exceedingly early in that universal struggle." He is attempting to imagine what his family members looked like based on their gravestones when an escaped convict named Abel Magwitch, "a fearful man, all in coarse gray, with a great iron on his legs," sneaks up and seizes Pip by the chin. Magwitch is "soaked in water, and smothered in mud, and lamed by stones, and cut by flints and stung by nettles, and torn by briars," and above all, he is starving. He threatens to tear out Pip's heart and liver, or worse, eat his "fat cheeks," unless he brings him food and a file to cut the iron from his legs. Pip promises he will bring him both things the next day and rushes home to his sister's house, where more terror awaits him.

Pip's sister, Mrs. Joe Gargery, is a "tall and bony" nightmarish figure, "with black hair and eyes, [and] such a prevailing redness of skin that [Pip] sometimes used to wonder whether it was possible she washed herself with a nutmeg-grater instead of soap." Feeding her husband and Pip is not an act of love for Mrs. Gargery, but rather something that she holds against them, reminding them always of how often she is forced to wear her apron. She cuts their bread in "a trenchant way" and spreads the butter with "a slapping dexterity." It's no wonder Pip is absolutely terrified of stealing any food from her.

He keeps his promise to Magwitch, though, and as soon as "the great black velvet pall outside my little window was shot with gray," he sneaks downstairs and into the pantry. Despite having promised Magwitch only to get him "what broken bits of food" he could, Pip steals "some bread, some rind of cheese, about half a jar of mincemeat (which I tied up in my pocket-handkerchief with my last night's slice), some brandy from a stone bottle . . . a meat bone with very little on it, and a beautiful round compact pork pie." The pie is up on a high shelf, "put away so carefully in a covered earthenware dish in a corner." He takes it "in the hope that it was not intended for early use, and would not be missed for some time."

At dawn the next day, Pip runs through

the marshes toward the graveyard, imagining the whole way that the "gates and dikes and banks" were screaming, "A boy with Somebody-else's pork pie! Stop him!" Pip gives the food and brandy to Magwitch and watches sympathetically as he gobbles it all down. "Pitying his desolation, and watching him as he gradually settled down upon the pie, [Pip] made bold to say, 'I am glad you enjoy it.' "

Pip's kindness and generosity toward Magwitch change the course of both of their lives. Magwitch goes on to become a successful sheep farmer and stockbreeder, and puts all of his money away to send to Pip. It is Magwitch, not Miss Havisham, who makes it possible for Pip to become an educated gentleman, eventually worthy of Estella's love — all as a thank-you for that humble pork pie.

GREAT EXPECTATIONS

Pork Pie

Pork pies have a long and proud history in England. They are usually eaten cold, with cornichons, grainy mustard, a slice of cheese, and a good ale. You can get leaf lard from your butcher, or substitute vegetable shortening. (Do not buy the hydrogenated lard on supermarket shelves.)

Serves 8 to 10

Dough
1/2 cup rendered leaf lard, cubed and frozen
8 tablespoons (1 stick) unsalted butter, cubed and frozen
4 1/2 cups pastry flour
3/4 teaspoon kosher salt
1 cup ice-cold water
1 large egg
1 teaspoon cream

Filling
1 pound fresh pork trotters
8 ounces pork bones
2 yellow onions, quartered
2 carrots, halved
2 celery ribs, halved
1 bay leaf
1 teaspoon whole black peppercorns
3 quarts water
2 pounds boneless pork shoulder, cut into 1/4-inch cubes
8 ounces skinless pork belly, cut into 1/4-inch cubes
8 ounces mild slab bacon, cut into 1/4-inch cubes

1 1/2 teaspoons kosher salt, plus more to
taste
1/2 teaspoon freshly ground black pepper
1/2 teaspoon ground sage
1/2 teaspoon freshly grated nutmeg
1/8 teaspoon pink curing salt (optional)

Make the Dough:

Combine the frozen lard and butter, pastry flour, and salt in the bowl of a food processor and pulse until pea-sized meal forms. Transfer the meal to a large bowl and mix in the ice-cold water until a dough forms (you may not need the full 1 cup). Bring the dough together, being careful not to overwork it. Separate out two-thirds of the dough, flatten it into a disk, and wrap it in plastic. Do the same for the remaining one-third of the dough. Refrigerate both dough disks for at least 2 hours.

Make the Filling:

Combine the pork trotters, pork bones, onions, carrots, celery, bay leaf, and peppercorns in a large, heavy-bottomed stockpot and cover with the water. Bring to a boil over medium heat, then reduce the heat to medium-low and simmer for 1 1/2 hours.

After 1 1/2 hours, strain the stock through a fine-mesh sieve into a smaller pot, discard the cooked ingredients, and bring the stock to a boil over medium-high heat. Boil gently until it has reduced to 2 cups, about 30 minutes. Strain the reduced stock through a double layer of cheesecloth into a bowl, let it cool a bit, and then cover the bowl and place it in the refrigerator to chill completely.

In a large bowl, toss together the pork shoulder, pork belly, bacon, salt, pepper, sage, nutmeg, and pink curing salt (if using — it will help preserve the meat's pink color).

Assemble the Pie:
Preheat the oven to 350°F.

Take the larger dough disk from the refrigerator and turn it out onto a well-floured surface. Roll it into a circle 1/4 inch thick. Line the bottom and sides of an 8-inch springform pan with the dough and fill the crust with the meat and spice filling.

Roll the smaller dough disk into a circle 1/4 inch thick, and cut out a 1 1/2-inch circle from the center. Place the top crust over the filling and crimp the edges of the top and bottom crusts together until they are fully sealed.

Beat the egg and cream together and brush the crust with the egg wash. Bake for

30 minutes. Reduce the oven temperature to 325°F and bake for an additional 1 1/2 hours.

Place the pie on a wire rack to cool for 15 minutes. Once the pie has cooled slightly, reheat your cooled trotter stock to liquid (it will have set to a gel in the refrigerator). Use a turkey baster to begin filling the pie with the stock through the hole you cut in the top crust. Allow the pie to absorb the stock in between each addition, tapping it very gently and moving it around to let the stock soak into all the crevices. Once all of the stock is added, allow the pie to cool to room temperature before transferring it to the refrigerator to chill for at least 4 hours or preferably overnight, as you want the stock to gel. Slice and serve cold.

MOBY-DICK

CLAM CHOWDER

In the early 1970s my dad's parents bought a house on a tree-lined stretch of Hussey Street on Nantucket. Like most of the houses nearby, it had once been the house of a ship's captain. This one in particular supposedly belonged to a famous whaling captain. My grandparents converted it into an inn that they called the Grey Goose, where they spent many of their happiest years. My dad would spend summers there, working as a garbage man and picking up odd handyman jobs.

In those days, Nantucket was already populated by the super-wealthy, especially in the summertime, but it was the old, proper, New England kind of wealth that nobody talked about openly or flashed around. My grandfather was able to buy the inn on a high school principal's salary, which would be absolutely unheard of today. When my grandmother passed away in 1980, my grandfather sold the inn for next to nothing, too heartbroken to haggle and desperate not to be living alone in a place so much associated with their life as a couple.

Despite the fact that my grandfather sold the Grey Goose, we still went to Nantucket every summer when I was a kid. We rented the same cottage year after year and spent long days hunting for crabs, playing paddle-ball, and swimming in the chilly, black ocean. At night, my dad read *Moby-Dick* to my sisters and me, telling us that Captain Ahab was actually the old whaling captain who had lived on Hussey Street. My dad was always happiest on these vacations. I think he felt his parents' spirits most clearly on the island.

When I was ten or eleven we stopped going to Nantucket. The island had changed to a point that my dad barely recognized it anymore, and the cottage that we always rented was sold and knocked down — it felt like the closing of a chapter.

It was nostalgia and a longing for that place and time that led me to pick up my dad's worn copy of *Moby-Dick* the summer before I entered college. I was astounded to discover how much of it I still knew by heart from all of the summers spent listening to it before bed. Herman Melville is so widely associated with Nantucket, and he so vividly captures the spirit of it in *Moby-Dick,* that it's nearly impossible to believe that when *Moby-Dick* was published in 1851 he had never set foot on the island.

Although Melville didn't know Nantucket firsthand, he knew the East Coast and the whaling life well enough from personal experience to write the book convincingly. His life at sea started in the summer of 1839, when he was twenty years old, as a "green hand" for a ship sailing from New York to Liverpool. In 1841 he joined the crew of a whaling ship called the *Acushnet* and sailed with them for eighteen months before deserting the ship in the Marquesas Islands, where he lived among the Typee natives for three weeks. He sailed with two other whaling ships after the *Acushnet,* partaking in mutinies and spending time in jail along the way.

Given my view of the world, I can't help but wonder if part of the reason for Melville's desertion and mutiny on these whaling voyages was the state of the meals on board. The food on whaling ships was often close to inedible — moldy, hard biscuits with bug-infested molasses and heavily salted dried horse meat were common fare, and there was little variety. It's no wonder that Melville, upon deserting the *Acushnet,* was so happy to be with the Typee, who ate fresh fruit, roasted suckling pigs, and even whole raw fish — bones, eyeballs, and all.

In the opening chapters of *Moby-Dick,* Ishmael spends his final nights before setting sail aboard the *Pequod* at the Try Pots Inn on Nantucket, preparing for his journey at sea. Part of this preparation, it seems, is enjoying one final good meal before the inevitable culinary wasteland that awaits him at sea, where "all your meals for three years and more are snugly stowed in casks, and your bill of fare is immutable."

The chowder served to him by the innkeeper, Mrs. Hussey, is so good he spends the rest of the chapter discussing it. The chowder "was made of small juicy clams, scarcely bigger than hazel nuts, mixed with pounded ship biscuit, and salted pork cut up into little flakes; the whole enriched with butter, and plentifully seasoned with pepper and salt." Besides the pounded ship biscuit — also known as hardtack, this was used as a thickening agent in the days when heavy cream wasn't as readily available — this chowder sounds just like the soup I grew up eating in New England. (I like to remind my New York friends that even Melville, who was from Manhattan, was clearly a fan of the New England style of clam chowder.)

MOBY-DICK

Clam Chowder

My dad's chowder is one of the things I look forward to most about being home, especially in the summertime when the seafood is freshest and the corn is extra sweet. He generally uses a spicy Portuguese sausage called linguiça, but that can be hard to find, so we'll stick to salt pork here and add a heavy dose of Tabasco at the end.

Serves 6

7 pounds littleneck clams
1/4 cup sea salt

1 teaspoon unsalted butter
4 ounces salt pork or bacon, cut into 1/4-inch pieces
1 large yellow onion, diced
2 celery ribs, diced
2 tablespoons all-purpose flour
Kernels removed from 2 ears sweet corn
4 medium-size starchy potatoes (such as Idaho or russet), scrubbed and cubed
1 bay leaf
Leaves of 4 thyme sprigs
1 cup heavy cream
Tabasco sauce
Kosher salt
Freshly ground black pepper
Oyster crackers, for serving

The night before you are going to make the chowder (or at least 4 hours before), place the clams in a large pot, cover them with water until they are submerged, add the sea salt, and put the pot, covered, in the refrigerator. If you can't fit a pot this big in your refrigerator, you can use very cold water and allow the clams to sit in the salted water at room temperature for 4 hours. This will allow the clams to spit out the sand that they are holding inside their shells so that you don't end up with a gritty chowder.

The next day, or after 4 hours, remove the

clams and rinse them with fresh cold water. Rinse the pot of any grit or salt, return the clams to the pot, and add 4 cups fresh water. Bring the water to a boil over medium heat and boil until the clams just begin to open up, 8 to 10 minutes.

As soon as they open, remove the meat from the shells over the pot, to make sure that any juice that comes out ends up back in the stock. Discard the shells and set the clams aside.

Pour the liquid that you boiled the clams in through a coffee filter or double layer of cheesecloth into a separate bowl. You should have about 5 cups of clam stock.

Rinse out the pot again and melt the butter in it over low heat. Add the salt pork and cook until all of the fat renders out and the meat is lightly crispy, about 7 minutes. Add the diced onion and celery and cook until the onion is translucent, about 5 minutes.

Whisk in the flour and cook until the flour is lightly toasted and smells fragrant, like a biscuit, 1 to 2 minutes. Whisk in the clam stock a little bit at a time until it is all incorporated. Add the corn kernels, potatoes, bay leaf, and thyme and simmer until the potatoes are fork-tender, 10 to 12 minutes.

Add the clams and whisk in the cream. Season with Tabasco, kosher salt, and pepper to taste, and serve with oyster crackers.

Down & Out in Paris & London

RIB-EYE STEAK

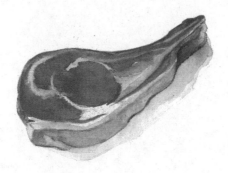

When I started working in restaurants as a student at NYU, I assumed that my two lives — my life studying English and Latin, and my life making and serving food — would be totally separate. I never expected that so much of my time in the kitchen would be spent talking to my coworkers about literature. Kitchens are physical places, and all of the chopping, sweating, tasting, poking, and bumping into each other naturally leads to a lot of bawdy, mindless chatter. In between all of the nasty jokes and posturing, though, in the quiet, reflective moments that kitchen work can also bring, we talked about books.

Of all the books I talked about in kitchens over the years, the one that came up most often was George Orwell's *Down and Out in Paris and London.* I had read *1984* and *Animal Farm* in high school, neither of which was particularly life-altering for me, but when Morgan, one of my favorite cooks, told me that *Down and Out* was the reason he first decided to set foot in a professional kitchen, I finally sat down and read it.

The thought of someone pursuing kitchen work *because* of this book still baffles me (Orwell's account of his backbreaking eighteen-hour days for pitiable pay is nearly unbearable at times), but I can certainly understand why someone accustomed to working in kitchens would love it. Orwell's descriptions of the frantic exhilaration of a dinner rush, of the feeling of emerging from the hatch into the cool night air after a fourteen-hour shift, of the camaraderie that exists between unlikely people in a kitchen and the satisfaction of a post–dinner service drink — these are all spot on. Orwell is young and hungry, and like so many of the people I've worked with over the years, he is cooking as a way to get by, and loving it.

One of the things that surprised me most when I first started cooking was the sheer amount of touching and shaping and tasting that goes into creating a dish. Even in the cleanest kitchens, I never worked with a chef who wore gloves. Chefs dip their tasting spoons into sauces more than once, they arrange the greens with their bare hands, they tidy the dots of sauce around the plate with their thumbs — it's very intimate. The kitchens Orwell was working in, and the cooks he was working with, were filthy, which makes the idea of this hands-on treatment slightly more stomach-turning, but the sentiment is still the same: "Food, to look smart, needs dirty treatment. . . . Roughly speaking, the more one pays for food, the more sweat and spittle one is obliged to eat with it."

According to Orwell, steak, which is often the most expensive item on a menu, is also among the most poked and prodded. In his experience, when a steak is brought to the head chef to be inspected before getting sent out, the chef "does not handle it with a fork. He picks it up in his fingers and slaps it down, runs his thumb round the dish and licks it to taste the gravy, runs it round and licks again." Right before the waiter comes for pickup, the chef gives the steak one final loving poke "with his fat, pink fingers, every one of which he has licked a hundred times that morning."

On a cooking line, the role of protein cook is highly regarded and is usually reserved for either the head chef or the head line cook. I think the same rule applies in a lot of home kitchens — the most skilled cook handles the meat — because there is a notion that it is the biggest, scariest, and most important job. From working at a butcher shop I've learned that a lot people are absolutely terrified of cooking meat. My coworkers and I spend a good amount of time talking people down from their pre–dinner party, picky-guest, former-vegan ledges, writing step-by-step directions in Sharpie on their paper-wrapped cuts of meat, seasoning their steaks, assuring them that they will have enough and that it will be delicious.

I'm not sure if it's the size, or the bone, or the price, but the steak that seems to terrify customers the most is the bone-in rib-eye, which also happens to be my favorite cut. I hope you'll let me take the fear out of the rib-eye for you. You don't even need a grill. The only tools you need are a well-seasoned cast-iron skillet and a meat thermometer.

Rib-Eye Steak
Serves 2

1 (1 1/2-pound) bone-in rib-eye steak, cut
   1 1/2 inches thick
Kosher salt
Freshly cracked black pepper
2 tablespoons high-smoke-point neutral oil,
   such as grapeseed oil
1 tablespoon unsalted butter

Pat the steak dry with a paper towel and leave it on the counter to sit out at room temp for 30 to 45 minutes prior to cooking. About 10 minutes before you're ready to cook, season the steak liberally on both sides with salt and pepper.

Heat the oil in a cast-iron skillet over medium-high heat until it just begins to smoke. Add the steak and cook until the surface has a good crusty sear, 6 to 8 minutes per side. For a steak cooked to just shy of medium (which is what I recommend for a rib-eye), the internal temperature should reach 135°F; the temperature will come up about 5 degrees while the steak is resting. Transfer the steak to a cutting board, put the butter on top to melt, and tent it with foil. Let the steak rest for about 10 minutes before slicing it against the grain and serving.

PRIDE & PREJUDICE
WHITE GARLIC SOUP

One of the questions I dread being asked most is "What's your favorite book?" It's not that I don't have an answer, or that my answer is always changing, or that it's some obscure book you've never heard of, it's just that my answer always seems to disappoint people a little bit. The fact is that *Pride and Prejudice* is my favorite book. There, I've said it. I've read it well over fifty times since my junior year of high school and have found something new to love about it on every single read. But somehow saying that it's my favorite book always feels kind of obvious, like saying Andy Warhol is your favorite artist, or *Adventures in Babysitting* is your favorite movie. (No? Just me?)

When I first read *Pride and Prejudice* at age sixteen, I knew nothing of Jane Austen's enduring influence and popularity. What I did know was that I was an American teenager, reading the book nearly two hundred years after its first publication, and not only did I understand it, but it was making me laugh out loud. This type of reading experience is at the core of what makes Austen extraordinary — that her wit and humor and portrayal of the human condition are still relatable and relevant, even cross-culturally.

There are many reasons that Austen has remained a household name while so many of her contemporaries — authors like Fanny Burney, Charlotte Lennox, and Eliza Haywood, who were also writing novels of social satire and domestic comedy — have fallen by the wayside. Austen's ability to write a fully realized and compelling story without burdening it with overly intricate details is a large part of her staying power.

As a reader, I never *feel* as if Austen's novels are lacking in detail because I can imagine her characters and settings so clearly, but if you actually go back and look for the particulars you will find only vague outlines. There is no lengthy description of Elizabeth Bennet's face, or the dress that Jane wore to the Netherfield ball. We never know Mr. Darcy's exact height, or just how beautiful the library at Pemberley really is — and yet we *see* all of these things in our heads so clearly. Austen allows us to build these details ourselves, to imagine elements of our own lives within the novel's confines, which is, I think, part of the reason that people feel so invested in and connected to her books.

This lack of specificity extends to food — Austen's novels are full of food and eating, but we rarely hear about any of it. The characters in *Pride and Prejudice* are forever sitting down to breakfast and commenting on how splendid their dinner was, they spar over luncheons and play cards after supper — but *what* are they eating? In her letters, Austen wrote constantly of the food she ate — lobster and asparagus, cheesecake, apple tarts, spareribs, rice pudding, pea soup, sponge cake — but in *Pride and Prejudice* she tells us only "the dinner was exceedingly handsome."

No matter how much I love *Pride and Prejudice,* I find its lack of food description *excruciating.* One scene in particular drove me crazy for years, and had me searching for Regency-era cookbooks whenever I went to the library. In the scene, Bingley tells his sister that he has decided to throw a ball at Netherfield, and that he will send out invitations "as soon as Nicholls has made white soup enough." What does this mean?! Why is time being measured by the creation of a really boring-sounding soup?! Curiously enough, I found the answer in Jane Grigson's *English Food* while looking for a recipe to make a traditional English-style cured ham for Austen's *Emma.*

White soup, it turns out, has a long history, dating back to medieval England and France, where it was served only in the wealthiest households. Given the aristocratic and courtly French origins of the soup, it seems that Bingley is saying that only the best will do for his finicky houseguests — Mr. Darcy, who is wealthy enough to keep a French cook, and Mr. Hurst, who prefers French cooking. Bingley's own humble English cook, Nicholls, will have to try her very hardest to impress these gentlemen, and as soon as she feels up to the task, they will have a ball. It's a small moment, one that is certainly not crucial to the plot, but understanding these small moments furthers our understanding of the world that Austen was writing about, which to me is important.

Recipes for white soup, sometimes called *potage à la blanc* or *soupe à la reine,* varied from kitchen to kitchen, but usually had a base of veal stock, cream, and almonds, and sometimes included bread crumbs, leeks, egg yolks, or rice. John Farley gives a recipe in his 1783 book *The Art of London Cookery:*

Put a knuckle of veal into six quarts of water, with a large fowl, and a pound of lean bacon; half a pound of rice, two anchovies, a few peppercorns, a bundle of sweet herbs, two or three onion [*sic*], and three or four heads of celery cut in slices. Stew them all together, till the soup be as strong as you would have it, and strain it through a hair sieve into a clean earthen pot. Having let it stand all night, the next day, take off the scum, and pour it clear off into a tossing-pan. Put in half a pound of Jordan almonds beat fine, boil it a little, and run it through a lawn sieve. Then put in a pint of cream, and the yolk of an egg, and send it up hot.

I tried this recipe, and any others I could get my hands on for white soup, and I'm sorry to tell you that I hated them all. The texture was funny, the almonds a little bit too sweet, the veal stock too jellied.

Before finding out what white soup actually was, I had spent years imagining what it could be — I thought maybe cauliflower or parsnip, potato and leek, or a fish chowder — and it's most likely because I had imagined all of these possibilities that the real soup didn't taste quite right to me. So, in the tradition of using our imaginations and filling in the blanks, as Austen so often asks us to do when reading her books, I've made a creamy, white garlic soup as a stand-in for the true almond and veal concoction. It's hardly courtly but it's certainly delicious — worth the risk that no one will want to kiss you at the ball after you've eaten it.

PRIDE AND PREJUDICE

White Garlic Soup
Serves 6 to 8

20 garlic cloves, peeled
2 cups whole milk
2 tablespoons olive oil
20 garlic cloves, unpeeled
2 tablespoons unsalted butter

1 small white onion, roughly chopped
Leaves of 5 thyme sprigs
4 cups chicken stock
1 cup heavy cream
Kosher salt
Freshly cracked black pepper
1/3 cup grated Parmesan cheese

The night before making the soup (or at least 4 hours before), put the peeled garlic cloves in a bowl, cover with the whole milk, cover the bowl, and place in the refrigerator. This will help leach out the bitter, spicy edge of the garlic. After the garlic has soaked overnight, discard the milk and reserve the soaked garlic cloves.

Preheat the oven to 350°F.

Combine the olive oil and unpeeled garlic cloves in a Dutch oven, cover, and roast until deeply golden brown, 30 to 45 minutes. Once the garlic cloves are roasted, squeeze them gently to remove them from their husks.

Heat the butter in a large stockpot over medium-low heat. Add the onion and thyme and cook until the onion is translucent, about 8 minutes. Add the chicken stock, cream, roasted garlic, and soaked raw garlic to the pot and increase the heat to medium. When the mixture comes to a gentle boil, lower the heat again and simmer for 5 minutes.

Remove the soup from the heat and transfer about one-third of it to a blender. (*Note:* Hot soup creates steam, and this steam has nowhere to go in a blender, which can lead to scary explosions if you don't follow this tip: On the lid of your blender there should be a hole that is covered by either a cap or a wand. Remove the cap or the wand and cover the hole with a clean kitchen towel. This gives the steam room to escape, which means the hot soup won't explode all over you.)

Blend the soup in batches until it is very smooth. Strain through a fine-mesh sieve, season with salt and pepper to taste, top with Parmesan, and serve.

THE SILENCE OF THE LAMBS

CROSTINI WITH FAVA BEAN AND CHICKEN LIVER MOUSSES

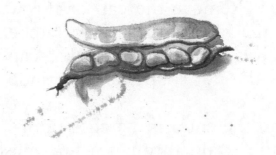

Every once in a while a literary recipe pops into my head and I have to ask myself, "Are you going too far?" This might be one of them, and the *porchetta di testa* is another, but I just can't help myself. Whenever I see fava beans in the market come spring, looking like the Arnold Schwarzenegger version of sugar snap peas, it's impossible for me not to think about Thomas Harris's Hannibal Lecter series. Was anyone else as obsessed with these books as I was in high school? (No? Is that why I had only one friend?)

224

Whether you've read the books or not, I'm sure you know a thing or two about Hannibal Lecter. Few other characters have had as lasting an impact and stayed as present in our cultural consciousness as Dr. Lecter. Thirty-two years after he first appeared in Harris's 1981 novel *Red Dragon,* he is the star of the NBC television show *Hannibal,* which premiered in May 2013.

The success of Harris's novels was due in large part to America's fascination with serial killers, a fascination that was new then but has only grown these last thirty years. Books and television are full of serial killers, from Chelsea Cain's Gretchen Lowell series and Roberto Bolaño's *2666* to TV's *Dexter, Criminal Minds,* and *The Mentalist.* Our culture is saturated with psychopaths. The criminal profilers that Harris was studying in the late 1970s were bringing to light a fact that we all know well now — that serial killers don't have to be scary-looking or visibly crazy, that most often they are in fact charming and well-spoken and sometimes even handsome. They could be law students or nurses or even brilliant psychiatrists.

Playing to America's morbid fascination with sociopaths, Anthony Hopkins's portrayal of Hannibal Lecter in the 1991 movie adaptation of *The Silence of the Lambs* helped secure the character's cultural staying power. It was the first horror film ever to win the Oscar for Best Picture, and only the third film ever to win Oscars in the top five categories — Best Picture, Best Actor, Best Actress, Best Director, and Best Writing.

Thanks to Hopkins, "I ate his liver with some fava beans and a nice Chianti" is as familiar a line as "Here's lookin' at you, kid." The quote is memorable not only because of that horrible sucking noise Hopkins makes after he says it, but also because of its eerie mix of savagery and refinement. Lecter is talking about cannibalizing someone, and yet his wine and side dish pairings are dead on. Liver and fava beans is a classic combination, and Chianti (in the book it's Amarone) complements both perfectly. Harris didn't throw in this line haphazardly; he knew food well, as did Dr. Lecter, who "was known for the excellence of his table and had contributed numerous articles to gourmet magazines."

Harris's agent once said of him, "He loves cooking — he's done Le Cordon Bleu exams — and it's great fun to see him in the kitchen while he prepares a meal and see that he's happy as a clam." His skill in the kitchen is probably the reason that he is able to make even the most disgusting food scenes sound somehow appealing. Dr. Lecter doesn't just eat brains, he "dredges them lightly in seasoned flour, and then in fresh brioche crumbs," he "adds shallots to his hot browned butter and at the instant their perfume rises he puts in minced caper berries," and then he "grates a fresh black truffle into his sauce and finishes it all with a squeeze of lemon juice." You could almost forget what it is you're reading about.

Almost.

My family ate a good amount of liver growing up, but I was embarrassingly old the first time I ever tasted a fresh fava bean. The only favas I had ever seen had already been shucked, blanched, peeled, and stuffed into rumpled bags in the freezer aisle, and those weren't even allowed in my house because of my dad's aversion to them. The first time I ever handled a fresh one I was working in a restaurant kitchen and the chef had put them on the menu as a special for that night, but they didn't arrive with the delivery until twenty minutes before service. Everyone was told to start shucking as quickly as possible so that they could be blanched and ready to serve by the time the first order came in.

All of the cooks gathered, hunched around

a table, burned and cut fingers moving like hummingbirds. I was so in awe of the beans I popped one in my mouth, uncooked and with the husk still on, and immediately spit it out. The cooks laughed mercilessly at me, but after service one of them handed me a heaping spoonful of the finished product — blanched and whipped into a mousse with lemon and garlic and Espelette pepper, the brightest green I'd ever seen.

THE SILENCE OF THE LAMBS

Crostini with Fava Bean and Chicken Liver Mousses
Makes 16 to 20 crostini

1 baguette
Fava Bean Mousse (recipe follows)
Chicken Liver Mousse (recipe follows)
Olive oil and/or port, for drizzling (optional)

Slice the baguette about 1 inch thick and toast the slices in a toaster oven or under a broiler. Top the crostini with dollops of fava bean mousse and/or cooled chicken liver mousse. Drizzle with olive oil or port if desired.

Fava Bean Mousse
Makes about 1 1/2 cups

1 1/2 pounds fresh fava beans
1/2 cup olive oil
1/3 cup freshly grated Parmesan cheese
Juice of 1/2 a lemon
1 tablespoon grated fresh lemon zest
1 garlic clove, minced
1/2 teaspoon kosher salt

Shell the fava beans from the pods and set them aside; you should have about 1 cup.

Bring a medium pot of water to a boil over high heat and prepare an ice bath (a large bowl of ice cubes and cold water). Boil the favas until they are tender and the outer skins begin to shed, 5 to 7 minutes. Drain and immediately place them in the ice bath (this stops them from continuing to cook and preserves their beautiful color).

Peel the outer membranes off the fava beans and discard them. Place the blanched and peeled favas and the rest of the ingredients in a blender and blend until very smooth.

Chicken Liver Mousse
Makes about 3 cups

2 tablespoons unsalted butter
2 tablespoons rendered chicken fat (or more
   unsalted butter)
2 small yellow onions, sliced
2 thyme sprigs
1 teaspoon black peppercorns
1/4 teaspoon ground cinnamon
1 piece star anise
1/2 bay leaf
1 pound chicken livers
1/8 teaspoon pink curing salt (optional)
1/3 cup ruby port
1 cup cream cheese, at room temperature
2 tablespoons sherry vinegar
1 tablespoon sugar
Kosher salt

Heat 1 tablespoon of the butter and 1 tablespoon of the chicken fat in a heavy-bottomed pot over medium heat. Add the onions and thyme and cook until the onions are golden brown.

Combine the peppercorns, cinnamon, star anise, and bay leaf in a spice grinder and pulse until finely ground (the cinnamon should already be ground, but adding it to the grinder helps the ingredients move around and get ground up). Add the spices to the onions and continue to cook until the onions are soft and caramelized.

Meanwhile, clean the chicken livers of any white or greenish fibers. (These fibers are safe to eat, but removing them will improve the texture of the finished mousse.)

Once the onions have cooked down, add the remaining tablespoon each of butter and chicken fat and raise the heat to medium-high. Add the livers and pink salt (if using — it will keep the livers from turning gray) and cook, stirring and tossing constantly, until they are firm to the touch but still rosy, 5 to 7 minutes. The internal temperature should be 165°F. (Generally, overcooking liver leads to an unappealing grainy texture, but the cream cheese and the blending/ passing through a sieve will help hide all manner of overcooking sins, which makes this process much less stressful.)

Discard the thyme sprigs and transfer the cooked livers and onions to a bowl. Deglaze the pan with the port and allow it to cook down for about 1 minute. Pour the reduced port over the livers and add the cream cheese.

In batches, blend the livers and cream cheese in a high-powered blender until very smooth. Pass the pureed liver mixture through a fine-mesh sieve into a bowl. Add the sherry vinegar, sugar, and salt to taste. Keep in mind that the flavor will change as the mousse cools, so add a little more salt than you think tastes right. Also feel free to add more sherry vinegar, sugar, and/or pepper.

Divide the mousse among three 8-ounce jars and top with a thin layer of rendered chicken fat (or olive oil) before placing the lids on. (This helps keep the liver fresh.) The mousse will keep for up to 10 days in the refrigerator.

MIDDLESEX

OLIVE OIL YOGURT CAKE

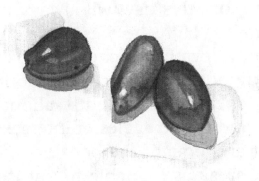

It was my grandfather Seymour (we call him "Papa") who suggested Jeffrey Eugenides's *Middlesex* to me over cups of egg and lemon soup at the Greek diner in my hometown. I think it must have been the book that made him want to eat there, because usually we went to Johnny's Luncheonette for breakfast, where a class photo of my mom and her twin sister hung on the wall and he could get a pastrami scramble with rye toast.

I was home from Brooklyn to celebrate

his eightieth birthday and had just started my blog a few months earlier. Papa was full of ideas about what books I should write about, but mostly he wanted to talk about *Middlesex,* which he had just finished a few days prior. I am impressed by my grandfather's kindness, intelligence, and open-mindedness pretty much every time I speak with him, but this day will always stand out in my mind. Here he was, an eighty-year-old man, a former butcher who had grown up in one of the toughest neighborhoods in Boston, speaking eloquently about gender identity and the struggles of intersex people.

I went and bought the book as soon as we finished breakfast. Unable to put it down, I read it over the course of only a few days. My grandfather was right, not only that it is a beautifully written and compelling story, but that it is filled with food. Cal Stephanides is born a girl in 1960 to a mother and father who are both first-generation Greek Americans. The Stephanides family, who formerly owned a diner that served typical American fare like cheeseburgers and milkshakes, eventually open a chain of hot dog stands called Hercules Hot Dogs. Inside of the Stephanides home, however, standard American food is not allowed, as Cal's mother, Tessie (who feels that her husband "is more in love with hot dogs than her"), believes that the grease will disrupt their digestion, and instead she insists on cooking them only traditional Greek foods.

Cal's grandmother Desdemona is living proof of the benefits of a Greek diet. At ninety-one years old she has "the arteries of a fifty-year-old," and shows no signs of slowing down. Impressed by her perfect health, a German doctor named Dr. Muller asks her to participate in a longevity study as part of the research he is doing for a medical journal article on the Mediterranean diet. Dr. Muller has denounced his German heritage when it comes to cooking, forgoing bratwurst, sauerbraten, and Königsberger Klopse and opting instead for Greek foods like "eggplant aswim in tomato sauce . . . cucumber dressings and fish-egg spreads . . . *pilafi,* raisins, and figs" because he believes in their power as "life-giving, artery-cleansing, skin-smoothing wonder drugs."

He asks Desdemona how much yogurt and olive oil she consumed as a child, and shares with her statistical graphs showing the life spans of other cultures — "Poles killed off by kielbasa, or Belgians done in by pommes frites, or Anglo-Saxons disappeared by puddings, or Spaniards stopped cold by chorizo." Much to the dismay of

Desdemona, who is more than ready to say her good-byes, the Greek lifeline keeps going and going.

Once Cal realizes the effect that the Mediterranean diet is having on her grandmother's body, she starts wondering how it might be affecting her own. At this point, Cal is twelve years old and still living as a girl. Over the summer, she has just become aware that all around her, girls are developing breasts and "growing modest," while she remains unchanged. She concludes that the Mediterranean diet that is keeping her grandmother alive against her will must also be to blame for her painfully slow sexual maturity. It must be, she thinks, the olive oil that her mother drizzles over everything that is keeping her body from changing, or the yogurt that she has for breakfast every morning that is stalling her breast development.

As readers, we know from the start that olive oil and yogurt are not the reasons for Cal's slow development. Eugenides has told us that the real culprit is 5-alpha-reductase deficiency, a condition that caused both doctors and Cal's parents to mistakenly identify him as a girl when he was born, based on his external anatomy. You would think that a story about a condition so rare would be difficult for most readers to relate to, but the genius of Eugenides's storytelling in *Middlesex* is that he makes Cal's story, and his struggle, accessible. Some readers will connect more with Calliope, the awkward preteen girl who is confused about the changes happening (and not happening) to her body, who feels freakish and lonely and left behind. Some will relate more to Cal, the forty-one-year-old man, falling in love with a woman and wondering if he will be enough, or too much, for her. Most everyone will relate to a character who is imperfect and insecure, who tries to find humor in tragedy, and who wants, above all, to be loved.

MIDDLESEX

Olive Oil Yogurt Cake
Serves 8

1 1/2 cups plain full-fat Greek yogurt
2/3 cup olive oil
3 large eggs
1 1/4 cups sugar
3/4 teaspoon pure vanilla extract
Juice and zest of 1 small orange
2 1/2 cups all-purpose flour
2 1/2 teaspoons baking powder

3/4 teaspoon baking soda
1/2 teaspoon kosher salt
1/4 cup raw almonds, roughly chopped

Preheat the oven to 350°F. Grease a 9-inch springform pan, line the bottom with a parchment paper circle, and grease the parchment.

In a large bowl, whisk together the yogurt, olive oil, eggs, sugar, vanilla, and orange juice and zest. In a separate bowl, whisk together the flour, baking powder, baking soda, and salt. Add the dry ingredients to the wet, mixing until a smooth batter forms. Pour the batter into the prepared pan and scatter the almonds over the top.

Bake until a toothpick inserted into the center comes out clean, about 45 minutes. Let the cake cool slightly before serving, or cool it completely and eat it cold.

BRIDESHEAD REVISITED
BLINIS WITH CAVIAR

A few years ago I was visiting my family for Christmas and my parents and I were trying to find something to watch on television. My sisters had long since disappeared upstairs to watch *The Real Housewives of New York,* so we felt free to let our dork flags fly. My dad pulled out his boxed set of videocassettes from the 1981 version of *Brideshead Revisited* and started to reminisce with my mom about how, in their first year of marriage, they used to wait all week for a new episode of the eleven-part miniseries to air, my dad rushing home from his job as a teaching assistant to make it in time. My mom found out she was pregnant with my older sister during the course of the miniseries, and she fell so in love with Lord Marchmain's levelheaded, insightful mistress, Cara, that she decided to name her next daughter after her (since Ande already had a name).

After hearing all of this I reluctantly decided to break my own rule of never watching a movie before reading the book. At first I wasn't sure about the movie — the opening is all noisy cannon fire and muddy 1980s colors — but soon Jeremy Irons's voice drew me in and I was hooked. I picked up my dad's old copy of the book that night and spent the rest of my visit reading the book during the day and watching the miniseries with my parents at night.

One thing the show couldn't hope to capture as well as the novel is Evelyn Waugh's beautifully descriptive food scenes, my favorite of which takes place when Charles Ryder has dinner with Rex Mottram. They eat a "soup of oseille, a sole quite simply cooked in white wine sauce, a caneton à la presse, a lemon soufflé," and "caviar aux blinis" whose "cream and hot butter mingled and overflowed, separating each glaucose bead of caviar from its fellows, capping it in white and gold." They eat happily to the sound of the duck press in the background — "the crunch of the bones, the drip of blood and marrow, the tap of the spoon basting the thin slices of breast."

I returned to Brooklyn after Christmas, just in time to work a dinner shift on New Year's Eve, followed by a brunch shift on New Year's Day, which also happens to be my birthday. As a baker, I had gotten used to never having my birthday off, since New Year's Day is one of the biggest brunch days of the year (resolutions be damned — hangovers need biscuits). So I slogged through my birthday brunch shift, feeling just the tiniest bit sorry for myself as I rolled brioche after brioche with my sticky, cramped fingers.

It finally came time, after a two-hour walk-in refrigerator deep clean, for me to leave. I was so exhausted that I didn't even notice that my bag was significantly heavier upon leaving than it was when I had left the house that morning. I got on the subway, opened my backpack to take out my book, and instead pulled out a huge bottle of champagne and a tiny tin of caviar left over from the New Year's Eve special the restaurant had run the night before. Attached to it was an order slip with "Happy Birthday!" written in scratchy handwriting and the signatures of all the cooks. Much to the horror and confusion of the woman next to me I actually burst into tears right there on the G train — total body exhaustion mixed with pure, unadulterated joy sometimes has that effect on me.

I had never eaten real caviar before, and I rushed home so quickly I almost cracked my head open on my icy stoop. I stepped out of my boots and, unable to help myself, ate two tiny spoonfuls standing in the kitchen in my coat and bare feet, wiggling my toes with each briny crunch, before finally deciding to give the caviar the respect it was due. Rex Mottram and those blinis . . . with their mingling of cream and hot butter and their sprinkling of chopped onions still on my mind, I immediately set to work whisking and frying, feeling lucky, and tired, and loved.

Blinis with Caviar

Makes 3 to 4 dozen

2 1/4 teaspoons active dry yeast (1 packet)
1/2 cup warm water (110°F)
3/4 cup all-purpose flour
1/4 cup buckwheat flour
1/2 teaspoon kosher salt
2 large eggs, separated (place whites in the refrigerator until ready to use)
1/2 cup buttermilk
1 tablespoon unsalted butter, melted and cooled, plus more for frying
1/2 teaspoon sugar
Caviar, crème fraîche, chopped red onion, and chopped fresh dill, for topping

Dissolve the yeast in the warm water in a small bowl and set aside until foamy, about 10 minutes.

In a small bowl, sift together the all-purpose flour, buckwheat flour, and salt.

In a large bowl, beat together the egg yolks, buttermilk, melted butter, and sugar. Mix the yeast-water mixture into the egg-buttermilk mixture. Now slowly pour the wet mixture into the sifted dry mixture and stir until smooth. Cover and place in a warm spot for 1 hour.

After about 50 minutes, beat the chilled egg whites to stiff peaks. Gently fold them into the batter.

Melt some butter in a medium skillet over medium-high heat. Using a 1-tablespoon scoop for consistent sizing, scoop the batter into the skillet. Fry until golden brown on each side and serve warm, topped with caviar, crème fraîche, chopped red onion, and dill.

The Corrections
CHOCOLATE CUPCAKES WITH PEPPERMINT BUTTERCREAM FROSTING

During my sophomore year in college, I worked mornings before class as a barista at a coffee shop in the West Village. Most of my opening shifts were with Elise, who was in her mid-twenties and had just moved to New York from Minnesota the year before. She had a wide, friendly face and sturdy calves. I felt safe and calm around her, as though everything in the world that needed doing that day would get done. Each morning, when the coffee urns let out their final, steamy gurgle-hiss, she would kneel down on the floor melodramatically and throw her head back and her hands in the air, thanking the coffee gods with a throaty laugh before pouring us each a mug. I liked her immensely.

Like lots of coffee shops in the city, we got our pastries from a commercial megabakery that churned out muffins and scones of completely uniform size, shape, and flavor. They were there every morning, waiting for us in large brown boxes stuffed precariously inside the store's metal grate, forever threatening to spill out onto the sidewalk as soon as we lifted them. The only times I ever saw Elise less than chipper were on the mornings that it was her duty to arrange the pastries in their wicker baskets. She ripped that box tape off like hot wax and shoved the sign-skewers into the scones as if they were voodoo dolls — it was positively aggressive, but I never had the nerve to ask her about it.

Finally, one slow day, we got to talking about what we did outside of work and school, and what we ultimately wanted to do. Elise told me that she had moved to

New York with the hopes of selling her homemade pastries to shops around the city. For nearly a year, though, she had been watching her savings dwindle while she battled with licensing offices that, for reasons I still can't entirely understand, wouldn't allow her to sell anything made in her Lower East Side apartment to the public.

It was Elise's grandmother, a German immigrant who had moved to Minnesota in the 1950s, who had taught her to bake. Elise called her "the only culinary bright spot in an otherwise bleak midwestern foodscape" — a phrase I memorized after writing it feverishly in my journal that night. She told me tales of foods I had never imagined: Jell-O pretzel salads, creamed chipped beef, sticky buns made with butterscotch pudding and dinner rolls, and city chicken — which wasn't chicken at all, but skewers of cubed, fried pork. Her grandmother's pastries were the only things she ate that didn't come from a can or a box. They were kneaded and punched and rolled by hand, and that meant a great deal to Elise.

The next day she brought me a box of her pastries and we sat on the counter and ate one of each with steaming mugs of black coffee in the quiet moments just before opening. There were plum kuchen, folded into flaky, palm-sized triangles, and savory hand pies (she used the British term "pasties") heavy with smoky ground sausage. There were silver-dollar-sized spirals of yeast dough, dripping with honey and studded with spiced walnuts, and fat, crispy donuts slathered in sour cream icing. In the box, too, there was a book, Jonathan Franzen's *The Corrections.* "Read this," she said, chewing her donut carefully. "It will prove to you I'm not lying about what I ate growing up." She turned to a dog-eared page and pointed to a circled sentence describing a salad of "water chestnuts and green peas and cheddar-cheese cubes in a thick mayonnaise sauce." I suddenly felt even more grateful for the flavorful kuchen I was cradling in my palm.

Having never spent an extended period of time eating in the Midwest, I can't say for sure if Elise and Jonathan Franzen weren't both exaggerating, but there is no doubt that *The Corrections* is a novel absolutely haunted by food. Enid Lambert, the deeply unsatisfied matriarch of the Lambert family, wields her power the only way she can — through the meals she serves her husband and children. When her husband forgets to say good-bye to her one morning on his way to work, she throws all of her anger and bitterness into dinner, creating for him a meal so vile it is referred to as "The Dinner of Revenge." It consists of "ferrous lobes of liver" dredged in "brown grease-soaked flakes of flour," rust-colored bacon, boiled beet greens that "leaked something cupric," and mashed rutabaga that "expressed a clear yellowish liquid similar to plasma or the matter in a blister."

This hostile culinary environment affects each of the Lambert children differently, both as children and in their adult lives. As a child, Gary Lambert always eats all of his vegetables, even asking for seconds of those mashed rutabagas, which "had the texture and temperature of wet dog crap on a cool morning." He eats them not because he loves them, but because he sees pleasing his mother as a means of survival. At night, tucking him in, Enid fawns over him, calling him her "good eater" and making him promise that he will remain so.

As an adult, Gary builds the life he thinks he is supposed to build; he gets married, has children, and lives in a beautiful house, but he is on the verge of collapse. To Gary, it is important that his family gather around a meal together just as he did growing up in St. Jude, even though his wife, Caroline (who refuses to cook and accuses Gary of having an unhealthy relationship with food), asks him, "It's not important to me, it's not important to the boys, and we're supposed to cook for you?" At first, preparing his signature mixed grill for the family's dinner brings him great pleasure, but eventually it comes to represent everything that is horribly wrong with his life — all the repetition, "the eternal broiling, broiling of the damned."

Despite the fact that the youngest Lambert, Denise, was in Enid's womb when "The Dinner of Revenge" took place, it's pretty safe to assume that she experienced her fair share of equally disgusting dinners growing up. As an adult, Denise drops out of college and throws herself headlong into the back-breaking, unstable world of professional cooking. She rises fairly quickly to chef-stardom on the Philadelphia food scene, but pays for it dearly with eighty-hour weeks and a seemingly endless train of dysfunctional and destructive relationships. The restaurant world is fickle and unpredictable, and Denise worries constantly about being shown up by her competitors, by her business partner, by the architecture of the restaurant itself.

The foods she cooks are lovely, and a

testament to the fact that Franzen himself must know food well, but something is missing. Although Denise is obviously talented, you rarely get the sense that she is driven by her love of food and cooking; rather, she seems motivated by a compulsive need to be the best at something.

Of all the Lambert children it is Chip who gives Enid the most trouble over her cooking — which she can't help but take personally. Unlike Gary, Chip is unable to fake it through the fried liver and mashed rutabaga that night. His father cheers him on, eating most of the rutabaga for him and promising him an Eskimo Pie if he can just eat that last bite. He tries, but he can't force himself to swallow, and he is made to sit at the table for five hours — well past his bedtime — until he has that one more bite.

When we meet Chip as an adult, he is working a tenure-track professor job at an elite college and seems to have his life together. He is well published, dating a historian, and hosting lavish monthly dinners for his students, at which he serves "langoustines, or a rack of lamb, or venison with juniper berries, and retro joke desserts like chocolate fondue." After rejecting a number of advances from an attractive freshman named Melissa, Chip finds her at his door one night with a platter of cupcakes. He has just started making himself a dinner of haddock with broccoli rabe and acorn squash, but the cupcakes sitting on his counter — frosted with a buttery peppermint icing — keep taunting him, and finally he gives in.

Once Melissa has plied him with cupcakes, Chip is helpless against her advances. Almost immediately after the cupcake incident, he begins an affair with Melissa that ends disastrously, and he has to leave the college in a cloud of embarrassment and shame. It seems fitting in some way that Chip, the boy who was never given the Eskimo Pie he was promised for eating his liver, is brought to his knees by a cupcake. Any cupcake this good (or this *bad,* I suppose) is worth replicating.

THE CORRECTIONS

Chocolate Cupcakes with Peppermint Buttercream Frosting
Makes 2 dozen

1 cup unsweetened cocoa powder, sifted
1 teaspoon instant espresso powder
2 cups boiling water
3 cups all-purpose flour

2 teaspoons baking soda
3/4 teaspoon kosher salt
1/2 teaspoon baking powder
1 cup (2 sticks) unsalted butter, at room temperature
2 1/2 cups sugar
4 large eggs, at room temperature
1 1/2 teaspoons pure vanilla extract
Peppermint Buttercream Frosting (recipe follows)

In a medium, nonreactive bowl, whisk together the cocoa powder, espresso powder, and boiling water and let it sit until cool, about 20 minutes.

Preheat the oven to 350°F. Line two 12-cup cupcake tins with paper liners.

In a separate bowl, whisk together the flour, baking soda, salt, and baking powder and set aside.

In the bowl of an electric mixer fitted with a paddle attachment, beat the butter until smooth. Add the sugar and beat until light and fluffy, about 3 minutes. Add the eggs and vanilla and beat until incorporated, scraping down the sides of the bowl intermittently.

Alternate adding the flour mixture and the cocoa powder mixture to the butter and sugar, beginning and ending with the flour, until everything is mixed together and smooth (be careful not to overmix).

Pour the batter into the cupcake tins until they are two-thirds full.

Bake until a tester inserted into the center comes out clean, about 20 minutes. Turn the cupcakes out onto a cooling rack to cool completely before frosting.

Peppermint Buttercream Frosting
Makes about 4 cups

1 cup (2 sticks) unsalted butter, at room
  temperature
1/4 teaspoon kosher salt
5 cups confectioners' sugar, sifted
1 teaspoon pure vanilla extract
1 teaspoon pure peppermint extract
3 to 5 tablespoons heavy cream

In the bowl of an electric mixer fitted with a paddle attachment, beat the butter and salt on medium-low until smooth, about 1 minute. With the mixer running, slowly add the confectioners' sugar until it is fully incorporated, being sure to scrape down the sides after each addition. Lower the speed to low and add the vanilla and peppermint extracts and 3 tablespoons of the cream. If the frosting feels too stiff, add 1 to 2 tablespoons more. Bring the speed up to high and whip for a solid minute to get it nice and fluffy. Transfer the frosting to a piping bag and frost the cooled cupcakes.

THE AENEID

HONEY–POPPY SEED CAKE

When I was an English major at NYU, taking a foreign language was a much-grumbled-about requirement. Most students solved this grievance by taking introductory-level language courses for languages they had already taken throughout high school, hoping that it would earn them an easy A. The professors were hip to this scheme, though, and they made sure that the entry-level classes weren't actually entry-level at all, which meant that one week into my freshman year I was already heading toward a failing grade in my "entry-level" Italian class.

When I tried switching over to Spanish the same thing happened, so reluctantly I went back to Latin — the language I had been taking since seventh grade. There are forty thousand students at NYU, so I expected that there would be more kids in my college Latin class than there had been in my high school Latin classes. The first day of Latin, though, I walked into the classroom to see only six staring back at me.

What started as a requirement turned into one of the classes I looked forward to most. That small group and the professor became a family of sorts, and although we were required to take only a few semesters, I ended up studying Latin all four years of college. I was in my junior year when we started translating Virgil's *Aeneid,* and I had just broken up with the guy I had been dating since my senior year of high school. It was a hard breakup, if only because he was, at that point, my dearest friend and the greatest comfort I had in a city that still, after almost three years, didn't feel quite like home. We made the decision not to see or speak to each other for two whole weeks, just to let our feelings settle, and during that time *The Aeneid* became a salve for me.

The brainpower put toward translating it was the only thing that stopped my mind from wandering to loneliness and grief.

You don't have to be going through a breakup to be brought to tears by Dido's tragic love for Aeneas, but it certainly helps. I was a wreck through the entire translation of book four. I cried ugly, messy cries in the library cubicles and chugged Red Bulls in order to stay awake long enough to finish more translating, before falling into bed at two in the morning looking like a *more* disheveled Hagrid, but feeling somehow purged.

When Dido discovers that Aeneas, the man she considers to be her husband, is preparing his ship under cover of night to sail away from her forever, she (understandably) flies into a rage. Unlike me, forever thinking to myself, *I should have said that,* Dido is perfectly, bitingly eloquent, even in the midst of feeling "so totally devastated, so destroyed." Her parting words to Aeneas are some of the most powerful, and the most chilling, of any I have ever read:

I hope, I pray, if the just gods still have any power, wrecked on the rocks mid-sea you'll drink your bowl of pain to the dregs, crying out the name of Dido over and over, and worlds away I'll hound you then with pitch-black flames, and when icy death has severed my body from its breath, then my ghost will stalk you through the world! You'll pay, you shameless, ruthless — and I will hear of it, yes, the report will reach me even amongst the deepest shades of Death!

Aeneas sails away, and Dido decides she can no longer bear to live. She asks her sister, Anna, to build her a pyre so that she can burn all of the things that Aeneas has left behind, and tells her that she is going to see a Massylian priestess in order "to bring him back in love for me or free me of love for him." This priestess, Dido says, who "protected the golden apples / on their tree, and feasted the dragon / with morsels dripping loops / of oozing honey and poppies drowsy with slumber," has the power "to release the hearts of those she likes" and "to inflict raw pain on others." This, however, is not actually Dido's plan. Instead she "clambers in a frenzy / up the soaring pyre and unsheathes a sword." With "bloodshot eyes rolling, quivering cheeks blotched," she curses Aeneas one final time before falling onto the sword and into the pyre.

Only two chapters after Dido's tragic

death, the same honey-filled, poppy seed–studded cake makes another appearance, when the priestess leading Aeneas to the underworld throws Cerberus, the guard dog, "a sop, slumberous with honey and drugged seed / and he, frothing with hunger, three jaws spread wide, / snapped it up." Almost immediately, the drugged cake takes hold of the dog, and he lies down in a heap, allowing Aeneas and his party entry to the underworld. One of the first ghosts Aeneas sees is Dido, and he approaches her, weeping and asking for her forgiveness. But Dido, queen of the breakup, eloquent even in her silence, "turned away, her features no more moved by his pleas as he talked on / than if she were set in stony flint or Parian marble rock." She leaves Aeneas standing there, tears streaming down his face.

Even amid all of this tragedy, a cake "dripping loops of oozing honey and poppies" is not easy to forget. Unlike Dido, I never wanted to cause this man whom I had loved any pain; all I wanted was a distraction from the sudden quiet expanse of my foldout kitchen table. I made dozens of different honey–poppy seed cakes during those empty weeks, hoping to glean some of Dido's strength from them, or at the very least to get some sleep. I baked so many versions, in fact, that my copy of *The Aeneid* still has poppy seeds buried deep in its spine, and ten pages are now inaccessible, stuck together for eternity by honeyed fingerprints.

THE AENEID

Honey–Poppy Seed Cake

This recipe, which was written on the back pages of my well-loved copy of the book, is my favorite. It has a dense crumb and a serious dose of honey, and the poppy seeds provide just enough crunch, the lemon just enough brightness, to wake you from your drowsy, full-bellied stupor.

Makes 3 loaf cakes

3 1/2 cups cake flour
1 teaspoon baking powder
1 teaspoon baking soda
1/2 teaspoon kosher salt
1 cup (2 sticks) butter, at room temperature
1 1/2 cups sugar
1 cup honey
3 large eggs, at room temperature
1 cup brewed Earl Grey tea, warm but not
  hot
1/4 cup fresh lemon juice
2 teaspoons grated fresh lemon zest

1 1/2 teaspoons pure vanilla extract
1/4 cup poppy seeds

Preheat the oven to 350°F. Line the bottom of three 9-inch loaf pans with parchment paper. Grease the parchment and the sides of the pans, dust with flour, and tap out the excess.

In a medium bowl, whisk together the cake flour, baking powder, baking soda, and salt and set aside.

In the bowl of an electric mixer fitted with a paddle attachment, beat the butter until smooth. Add the sugar and honey and beat until light and fluffy, about 3 minutes. Turn the mixer to low and add the eggs, one at a time, mixing well after each addition.

Beat in the tea, lemon juice, lemon zest, and vanilla and mix until incorporated.

Slowly add the dry ingredients, scraping down the sides of the bowl, until everything is mixed in and the batter is smooth (be careful not to overmix).

Stir the poppy seeds into the batter with a spatula until they are spread throughout. Divide the batter evenly among the three loaf pans.

Place the pans on a baking sheet and bake until the center of each cake springs back when you touch it gently, and a toothpick inserted into the center comes out mostly clean (this is a sticky cake, so it won't be completely clean), 45 to 60 minutes.

Allow the cakes to sit for 20 minutes before turning them out onto a cooling rack. Allow them to cool completely before serving.

MRS. DALLOWAY
CHOCOLATE ÉCLAIRS

I have a complicated relationship with Virginia Woolf that dates back to an excruciatingly boring course I took on modernist writers while in college. Perhaps it was the oppressive fluorescent lighting and corrugated office ceiling in the lecture hall, or the professor's monotonous and uninspired rants, or the sea of students raising their hands to "ask questions," which really meant telling some pointless anecdote about their own lives — but I digress. Whatever it was, Virginia and I just did not get along.

The professor loved to use the words "otherworldly" and "ethereal" when describing Woolf, so much so, in fact, that the only fun part of the class was the collective eye roll that occurred whenever the words were repeated. One day, a student finally asked for an example of this ethereal otherworldliness, and the professor said, without missing a beat, "Have you ever noticed that there's hardly any food at all in any of her novels?"

It was at this point that I started to doubt that the professor had ever read any of the books he was teaching us — he was so terribly, terribly wrong. For all of my irritation and frustration with dear Virginia, her food scenes were actually among the main reasons I persevered through her novels. In *The Waves* we have Neville's beautiful roast duck, piled with vegetables, butter seeping through Bernard's crumpet, pheasant with bread crumbs and soft bread sauce, and Brussels sprouts with their "pungent, curious taste." In *To the Lighthouse* there is the *boeuf en daube* — the holy grail (or one of about seven) of all literary meals — a rich and tender stew of meats scented with "olives and oil and juice." This is one of four meals that most people mention first when I tell them that I write about literary food scenes; Miss Havisham's bride-cake, the banana breakfast in *Gravity's Rainbow,* and Bruce Bogtrotter's chocolate cake from *Matilda* are the others.

When it comes to Virginia Woolf and food, people also love to quote from *A Room of One's Own:* "One cannot think well, love well, sleep well, if one has not dined well." This quotation is everywhere on Etsy — embroidered on pillows, painted on clean white canvases, embossed on recipe note-books — and it points, these crafty folks seem to think, to Virginia Woolf's love of food. However, in context, the line refers to the women at the fictitious University of Oxbridge, who do not dine well, and as a consequence are not able to think, love, or sleep well.

Their dinner consists of transparent gravy soup, and a "homely trinity" of beef, greens, and potatoes, which Woolf describes as "the rumps of cattle in a muddy market." This is in stark contrast to the meal served to the male students at the same school, a meal of sole spread with cream, partridges with an array of salads and sauces, succulent young potatoes, and a dessert so good that "to call it a pudding and so relate it to rice and tapioca would be an insult."

The point is that Woolf's thoughts on eating could never be captured in a single quotation. There is always more going on behind the quote, surrounding it, and after it; this is due, in part, to the fact that Woolf herself had an incredibly difficult relationship with food. For the majority of her life, Woolf battled anorexia, or something resembling it, refusing to eat for long periods of time during bouts of depression and psychosis. Woolf's husband, Leonard, writes extensively about her "strange and slightly irrational attitude towards food" in his book *Beginning Again: An Autobiography of the Years 1911–1918,* referring to it as "this excruciating business of food."

Often, he had to sit by her side for hours at a time, coaxing her to eat just one meal, and worried that she would starve if left to her own devices. Some scholars speculate that Woolf's disordered eating was a reaction to having possibly been molested by her brother as a child; others, such as Madeline Moore, theorize that her refusal to eat was "one of Woolf's ascetic practices, adopted as a last-resort gesture of feminist political defiance." Leonard Woolf himself wonders if it wasn't simply "a (quite unnecessary) fear of becoming fat."

Of all the times Woolf writes about food

in her diaries, one of the most telling, to me, comes from an entry dated October 7, 1918, in which she recounts her revulsion at seeing the strangers around her at a restaurant eat. She describes watching them eat as staring into "the lowest pit of human nature," and seeing "flesh still unmolded to the shape of humanity." She wonders "whether it is the act of eating & drinking that degrades, or whether people who lunch at restaurants are naturally degraded."

Woolf's attitude toward food is Victorian, focusing on the grotesqueness of the flesh and the marrying of moral character with eating. It's an attitude most clearly displayed in the characterization of *Mrs. Dalloway*'s Miss Kilman, a history tutor and religious zealot who tries her hardest to denounce the worldly matters of the flesh, but finds that "food was all that she lived for." At tea, her student Elizabeth Dalloway can't help but observe Miss Kilman's unseemly greediness toward the offerings. At one point during their tea, Miss Kilman, who has been "eating, eating with intensity," gets upset when a child takes the pink sugared cake she had her eye on. Ever the victim, Miss Kilman sees it as an attack on her only happiness in life — her enjoyment of food.

In an attempt to force Elizabeth, with

whom she is in love, to stay with her at tea instead of leaving for her mother's party, Miss Kilman passive-aggressively "finger[s] the last two inches of a chocolate éclair" and tells Elizabeth, "I've not quite finished yet." When it becomes clear that Elizabeth is itching to go, Miss Kilman ever so slowly lifts the éclair to her mouth and swallows it down with the dregs of her tea. She is despondent after this lunch, certain that Elizabeth has turned on her, is repulsed by her — and we as readers can't blame Elizabeth for feeling that way. By simply placing a plate of sugared cakes and chocolate éclairs in front of her, Woolf is able to speak volumes about Miss Kilman's character and, we can infer, about her own repulsion at watching people eat.

Psychological and textual analysis aside, I understand Miss Kilman. I can't say in all honesty that I wouldn't be upset if a kid took the last pink sugared cake at my tea party, and I would be lying if I told you that immediately after reading this scene in class, my friend Emily and I didn't go straight to Pasticceria Rocco and get two big, fat chocolate éclairs.

Chocolate Éclairs

Because of their fancy French name, the idea of making chocolate éclairs at home may seem intimidating at first, but actually it's simple — a quick *pâte à choux* (again, don't be scared by the French), a rich vanilla pastry cream, and some good-quality tempered chocolate, and you are in business.

Makes 10 to 12 éclairs

Pastry Cream
1 cup whole milk
1 cup heavy cream
2 vanilla beans, seeds scraped out and pods reserved
6 large egg yolks
2/3 cup sugar
Pinch of kosher salt
1/4 cup cornstarch
1 tablespoon unsalted butter, cold

Pâte à Choux
1 cup water
8 tablespoons (1 stick) unsalted butter
1 tablespoon sugar
1/4 teaspoon kosher salt

1 cup all-purpose flour
4 large eggs, lightly beaten
1 large egg beaten with 1 1/2 teaspoons
water, for egg wash

Chocolate Glaze
1/2 cup semisweet chocolate, coarsely
chopped
1/2 cup heavy cream

Make the Pastry Cream:
Prepare an ice bath by filling the sink or a very large bowl with ice cubes and cold water. Place a large glass or metal bowl over the ice bath and set a fine-mesh strainer over the bowl.

Combine the milk, cream, and vanilla seeds and pods in a medium heavy-bottomed saucepan and bring to a simmer over medium heat. Once the mixture comes to a simmer, take it off of the heat and set aside for 15 to 20 minutes to infuse.

In a large bowl, whisk together the egg yolks, sugar, and salt until they are airy and light in color. Whisk in the cornstarch until it is smooth.

Take 1/4 cup of the milk-cream mixture and slowly drizzle it into the yolk-cornstarch mixture, whisking constantly so that the yolks don't scramble. Repeat with the remaining hot milk and cream. Discard the vanilla bean pods and return the mixture to the saucepan.

Cook over medium heat, whisking constantly, until the temperature reaches 160°F. The mixture will be thick, with large bubbles rising to the surface and slowly bursting.

Strain the pastry cream through the fine-mesh strainer into the bowl set over the ice bath. Whisk in the cold butter. Whisk the mixture until it has cooled to room temperature. Place plastic wrap over it, pressing it flush to the surface of the pastry cream so that it doesn't form a skin, and set it in the refrigerator to chill for 2 hours.

Make the Pâte à Choux:
Preheat the oven to 400°F. Line two baking sheets with parchment paper.

In a large, heavy-bottomed saucepan, heat the water, butter, sugar, and salt over medium heat until the butter is melted and the water is simmering.

Add the flour all at once and mix it with a wooden spoon until it is fully incorporated into the liquid. The mixture will be very stiff. Keep stirring it over medium heat until the batter loses its shine. The batter will get even stiffer, and feel more like a loose bread dough. This will take about 4 minutes of continuous stirring.

Transfer the dough to the bowl of an electric mixer fitted with a paddle attachment. Mix at medium speed for 1 minute.

After 1 minute, slowly add the 4 beaten eggs to the batter until they are fully incorporated and the batter is again glossy and smooth. When you lift the paddle out of the batter, it should fall back into the bowl in slow ribbons.

Fill a pastry bag fitted with a 1-inch plain tip with the batter and pipe out oblong shapes (about 5 inches long and 1 inch wide) onto the lined baking sheets, spacing them at least 2 inches apart — you should get 10 to 12.

Gently brush the tops of the éclairs with the egg wash. Then, dip a fork into the egg wash and gently drag it across the surface of the éclairs — this will help the éclairs rise evenly.

Bake for 15 minutes, then reduce the heat to 325°F and bake until golden brown all over, 25 to 30 more minutes. Turn off the oven and allow the éclairs to cool in the oven for 10 minutes before taking them out and letting them cool further on the baking sheet.

Make the Chocolate Glaze:

Place the chocolate in a large glass bowl and set aside. Heat the cream in a small saucepan over medium-low heat until just before boiling — steam should be rising from the surface and tiny bubbles should be forming around the edge. Pour the hot cream over the chocolate and allow it to sit for 30 seconds before whisking until smooth.

Assemble the Éclairs:

Once the éclair shells and the pastry cream have cooled, insert a long skewer through one end of each éclair, making sure not to poke it through the other side, and move it around to make space for the pastry cream.

Fill a pastry bag fitted with a filling tip with pastry cream and pipe it into the éclairs until they are full but not about to burst. Dip the top of each éclair in the chocolate glaze and set it on a parchment-lined baking sheet. Repeat with the remaining éclairs. Set them aside until they have cooled and set, 1 to 2 hours.

Anna Karenina

OYSTERS AND CUCUMBER MIGNONETTE

In my junior year of college, I took an American literature class — a huge bleacher-seated lecture with 250 sleepy, hungover kids. Looking back on these days, I recall there was almost always someone who stood out in these big auditorium classes, not necessarily as the smartest, but certainly as the *coolest.* In this particular class it was Ruthie, a pixie-boned girl with sallow skin and unkempt, dyed-black curls that sprung from her head like an overgrown houseplant.

Ruthie smoked Sobranie Black Russians, one of which was always tucked behind her ear, the gold tip gleaming out of her curls. She introduced herself on the first day of our recitation by announcing in a bored voice that she was taking the course as a requirement, that her actual area of study was Russian literature with a focus on Leo Tolstoy's moral writings. I had no idea what that meant, but it sounded so much cooler than "I'm studying English and Latin." No matter how cold it was, Ruthie wore slouchy black tank tops to expose a tattoo on her right arm — a strikingly realistic portrait of Tolstoy, heavily shaded in deep grays and blacks. Underneath it was a quote in typewriter font that I spent the entire semester trying to make out; it read: "Don't steal fresh bread."

I had, in those days, a deep-seated dislike of Russian literature, stemming from an earlier dark period in high school in which I was assigned *Crime and Punishment, The Death of Ivan Ilyich,* and the similarly titled and equally depressing *One Day in the Life of Ivan Denisovich.* I walked around for weeks with a gray hollowness in my gut after reading those books, and vowed I would never read any Russian literature again, but Ruthie's tattoo haunted me. I was frantic to know what it meant. Apparently, so were other students in class, because finally, on the last day of recitation, a group of them worked up the nerve to ask. She gave the subtlest eye roll and said, "It's complicated. It's from *Anna Karenina,*" before packing up her bag and lazily sauntering out.

When I think about Ruthie now, it's not with fondness, but I do owe her a thank-you for lifting my self-imposed ban on Russian literature. Immediately after class that day I went and bought a copy of *Anna Karenina* and tore into it, intending only to find the source of Ruthie's tattoo, but I became so engrossed that I finished it in just under two weeks. I loved the book, not only because it was beautifully written, and tragic, and epic, but also because of the heavy symbolism attached to every scene involving food and eating — perhaps the most famous of which was quoted on Ruthie's arm.

Early in the novel, Tolstoy gives readers a glimpse into the moral character of two of the novel's leading men, Konstantin Levin and Stepan Oblonsky, by showing us what, and how, they eat at a restaurant. Oblonsky handles the ordering, making it clear not only that he has a large appetite, but also that he is used to eating in fine restaurants. He demands "two, or no, that's not enough, three dozen oysters, vegetable soup . . . then turbot with a thick sauce, then roast beef, but see to it that it's all right. Yes, some capon, and lastly, some preserve," and as an afterthought he tacks on a bottle of Chablis and some Parmesan cheese.

Levin, who lives the simple life of a landowner and farmer, is uncomfortable during Oblonsky's exchange with the waiter; he feels "out of his element in this restaurant, amid the confusion of guests coming and going, surrounded by the private rooms where men and women were dining together; everything was repugnant to his feelings — the whole outfit of bronzes and mirrors, the gas and the Tatars." More than that, though, he fears that by participating in such lavishness, "the sentiment that occupied his soul would be defiled."

He tells Oblonsky that what he would really like is some *shchi* — a humble cabbage soup — or *kasha,* a simple buckwheat porridge, and eats his oysters hesitantly, wishing instead for cheese or white bread.

When he realizes that Oblonsky is disappointed that he is not enjoying himself more, Levin explains, saying, "In the country we make haste to get through our meals so as to be at work again; but here you and I are doing our best to eat as long as possible without getting satisfied, and so we are eating oysters."

Unlike Levin, Oblonsky devours his oysters in a way that is suggestive of his insatiable sexual appetite. He tears "the quivering oysters from their pearly shells with a silver fork and swallow[s] them one after another," his eyes "moist and glittering" with satisfaction. "The aim of civilization," he tells Levin, "is to translate everything into enjoyment," to which Levin responds, "If that is its aim, I should prefer to be a savage." Levin responds in a similar manner when the notion of infidelity comes up later on, telling Oblonsky (a known adulterer) that cheating is like emerging full from dinner and then stealing a loaf of bread from a bakery. Oblonsky replies, "Bread sometimes smells so good, that one cannot resist the temptation," and asks, "What is to be done?" Levin answers simply, "Don't steal fresh bread."

For Levin, food and morality are closely linked, and the same was true for Leo Tolstoy. While Tolstoy was writing *Anna Karenina* in the 1870s, he was also undergoing a major spiritual transformation, a significant aspect of which included becoming a strict vegetarian. Tolstoy wrote passionately about his renunciation of "flesh-meat" in several essays, detailing the horrors of nineteenth-century Russian slaughterhouses, and speaking to farmers and butchers about the impact that killing and eating animals had on their spirit. Tolstoy believed that eating meat was not only immoral, because of the suffering it caused other living creatures, but that it blocked man's path to spiritual enlightenment by suppressing his capacity for "sympathy and pity toward other living creatures like himself."

Of all the food in Oblonsky and Levin's dinner that is ripe for re-creating — vegetable soup, turbot in a thick sauce, roast beef and capon — I chose to focus on the oysters because of their complicated moral standing in the world of vegetarianism and veganism. A handful of the vegans and vegetarians I know eat oysters because, they argue, they are biologically indistinguishable from plants in that they cannot feel pain and are not motile. They argue also that farming them has little to no impact on the environment, and can actually be beneficial for water quality. Other vegans and vegetarians maintain that this is a ridiculous position, that oysters are living creatures and therefore should not be consumed. It's an interesting debate, and I sincerely wish we could have gotten Tolstoy's view on it. For now, though, let's conjure Oblonsky, for whom eating is "one of the pleasures of life," and enjoy these oysters.

ANNA KARENINA

Oysters and Cucumber Mignonette

Makes 3 dozen oysters with sauce

1 cup champagne vinegar
2 teaspoons sugar
1/4 teaspoon kosher salt
1 cup minced shallots
1 cup peeled and finely minced hothouse cucumber
1 1/2 teaspoons coarsely ground black pepper
36 oysters, shucked

In a large, nonreactive bowl, whisk the champagne vinegar, sugar, and salt until they are completely dissolved. Add the minced shallots, cucumber, and pepper and mix to combine. Spoon onto oysters and enjoy.

■ ■ ■ ■

PART 3
ADULTHOOD

■ ■ ■ ■

THE BLUEST EYE
CONCORD GRAPE SORBET

When I moved to Brooklyn what feels like ten lifetimes ago, it was the hottest, thickest part of July. An ominous black mold crept across the ceiling in the bathroom of my new apartment like sponge paint, thriving in the dense humidity. In the kitchen, my feet stuck to a mysterious blue substance that no amount of elbow grease could remove, and there were cockroaches, droves of them, their burned sugar shells lounging in the drains and scurrying across the walls. (Sorry I never told you this, Mom and Dad.)

The first night there was a ground-shaking thunderstorm — not the kind that you cuddle up against, but the kind that actually terrifies you. I bought a frozen pizza and a bottle of wine, only to remember that the gas hadn't yet been turned on, so I couldn't use my oven, and I had left my wine key behind in my former apartment. I bought a honey-dipped donut from the deli next door, sat on the gray-blue carpet of my bedroom floor, and cried myself exhausted.

The next morning I pulled myself out of bed early and immediately set to scrubbing, scraping, and bleaching. When I opened my kitchen window to air out the smell of cleaning chemicals, I noticed for the first time a delicate green vine creeping and curling along the bricks of my building and wrapping itself around the fire escape. Even though it was too early for the plant to bear any fruit, I recognized it immediately as a Concord grapevine.

There was a house on the street where I grew up that was covered on one side with

Concord grapevines, and my friends and I spent many a crisp fall afternoon gorging ourselves on the grapes. They are one of the only fruits that truly taste like their artificial imitation, which is one of the reasons I loved them so much as a kid — they tasted like Welch's grape jelly and purple Bazooka gum. Eating them always felt like something I shouldn't be doing (and seeing as I was stealing them from a neighbor's yard, that feeling was probably valid).

Maybe it's from the five months I spent in college writing a paper on food imagery in Toni Morrison novels, but I rarely eat grapes without thinking of her. Nobody can make produce sexy quite like Morrison can — her plants sway their hips, her fruits swell and bloom, her berries run over with juice. Grapes make an appearance in almost all of her novels — in *Beloved* there is Mr. Garner's grape arbor, which yields "grapes so little and tight. Sour as vinegar too." In *Song of Solomon* Pilate makes wine from piles of grapes and the women eat the leftovers with hot bread and butter. In *Paradise* statues of Christ and the Virgin Mary are strangled by overgrown grapevines, and in *Jazz* there is Treason River, surrounded by hills covered in wild grapes.

My favorite of all of Morrison's grape passages, however, takes place in *The Bluest Eye,* when Cholly and Darlene chase each other through a field of muscadine, tossing the grapes at each other and lying down, their mouths "full of the taste of muscadine, listening to the pine needles rustling loudly in their anticipation of rain."

The grapes in this passage are ripe with possibility and promise — tasting their sourness is simply a reminder of what sweetness will eventually come. When I started seeing Concord grapes in the market a few weeks ago, I immediately thought of this book and that lonely, homesick time that feels so long ago now, when the grapes outside my window signaled to me not only respite from the heat of summer but also a time when my apartment might finally feel like my home.

The grapes on my fire escape are long gone now — my crazy landlord came at them with a weed whacker one day, convinced they were causing a bee infestation (I cried then, too), but my excitement over seeing them in the market hasn't faltered. This sorbet is a perfect way to enjoy their sweet, musky flavor. The lemon cuts the grapes' sweetness, and the wine makes their flavor a little more grown-up than the grape Popsicles of childhood. It is perfect on its own, in a cocktail, or sopped up with olive oil cake.

THE BLUEST EYE

Concord Grape Sorbet

Corn syrup keeps ice crystals from forming in the sorbet. If you don't mind the crystals, you can use 6 tablespoons mild honey instead.

Makes about 1 quart

2 1/2 pounds Concord grapes, stemmed and seeded (you can seed them in a food mill or a cherry pitter, or by hand with a knife)
1/2 cup corn syrup
1/4 cup dry red wine
Juice of 1/2 a large lemon

Place the grapes in a food processor and blend until they form a smooth pulp. Transfer the pulp to a piece of cheesecloth set over a bowl and wring them out until all of the juice is released. Whisk the corn syrup, red wine, and lemon juice into the grape juice. Transfer the liquid to a small saucepan and cook over medium heat until the mixture just comes to a boil, about 5 minutes. Chill the base thoroughly and spin according to the ice cream maker's instructions.

A Confederacy of Dunces
JELLY DONUTS

As kids, when my sisters and I were bored at church, we would write notes to each other on prayer cards with the stubby pencils tucked in front of the pews. Forty percent of it was pure nonsense — doodles and made-up words and outlandish "would you rather" scenarios. The other sixty percent of the time we asked each other simply, "If you could eat anything in the world at this very moment, what would it be?"

We answered from the depths of our stomachs, listened to our literal gut reactions, wrote the answers down earnestly, and passed the prayer cards back. At first, our cravings changed from moment to moment, swinging willy-nilly from fried chicken to Sour Patch Kids and getting progressively less coherent as our tights got itchier and our stomachs grumbled more loudly. Eventually, though, the game got boring. It wasn't that we ran out of foods to dream up, it was just that we had all settled on our favorites — our "desert island foods," as we called them. Mine was always mashed potatoes with cheddar cheese, Gemma always said extra-crispy French fries, and Ande always, *always* wanted a warm jelly donut.

Donuts are and always have been one of my favorite foods. Growing up I generally opted for the cake variety. I found it hard to determine whether yeasted donuts actually tasted like anything, or if all I was tasting was their filled centers. Jelly-filled in particular was always my least favorite donut — I found the squidgy center disconcerting and the jelly overly sweet and alarmingly red. It wasn't until I was an adult that I realized the error of my ways — the most significant of which was that I had only ever tried a

Dunkin' Donuts jelly donut. A few years ago, around Hanukkah, my friend took me to the neighborhood where he grew up in Borough Park, Brooklyn, and brought me to Weiss Kosher Bakery, home of the "heartburn-free donut," the best *sufganiyot* I've ever had.

Weiss's sells about 40,000 donuts during Hanukkah, a staggering number, especially if you've seen their ancient Hobart mixer and two-at-a-time filling-stuffer. I ate so many of those airy, raspberry jelly–filled delicacies that day that I had to curl my knees up to my chest and fall asleep on the subway ride home.

The cruelest part of the story is that despite how sick I was that night, I still woke up craving those jelly donuts the next morning. Lying in bed, all I could think about was how dangerously close I was to becoming Ignatius J. Reilly, the gluttonous main character of John Kennedy Toole's posthumously published novel, *A Confederacy of Dunces*. There has hardly ever been a more repulsive and unlikable antihero than Ignatius.

Walker Percy, who was instrumental in getting *A Confederacy of Dunces* published eleven years after John Kennedy Toole committed suicide, called Ignatius a "slob extraordinary, a mad Oliver Hardy, a fat Don Quixote, a perverse Thomas Aquinas rolled into one." He is lazy and selfish and, at thirty years old, still living with his mother, whom he treats like his personal waitress. While hot dogs are Ignatius's "desert island food," he is also a huge fan of jelly donuts. Early on in the book Ignatius casually mentions that he loves jelly donuts, and his mother immediately rushes out to a shop on Magazine Street in New Orleans and buys him *two dozen* of them. He eats nearly all twenty-four and sucks the jelly out of the ones he doesn't eat. The passage is one of the first glimpses into how unhealthy Ignatius's relationships with both food and his mother are.

When Patrolman Mancuso comes over, Ignatius's mother offers him a donut from the ravaged, grease-stained donut box, which "looked as if it had been subjected to unusual abuse during someone's attempt to take all of the donuts at once." All that is left inside the box are "two withered pieces of donut, out of which, judging by their moist edges, the jelly had been sucked." Not surprisingly, Patrolman Mancuso passes on the offer.

Don't let Ignatius's (or my) gluttony deter you — you need to make these donuts.

Jelly Donuts

Be forewarned that this is not a quick recipe. It takes some planning, but it's really worth it. The long rise in the refrigerator gives the yeast time to ferment, which will give the donuts a wonderful flavor and texture. Whenever I make yeast donuts I like to first make what's called a "yeast sponge," which you will see in the first part of the recipe instructions. This is a concentrated yeast dough that ferments on its own for a couple of hours before being added to the main dough. It's a game changer as far as donut making goes; it ensures that the delicious yeasty flavor of the donut will overpower the flavor of fry-oil and jelly.

Makes 30 to 40 small (2-inch) donuts

Yeast Sponge
2 1/4 teaspoons (1 packet) active dry yeast
  (not instant)
1/4 cup warm water (110°F)
1/4 cup pastry flour

Donuts
2 1/4 teaspoons (1 packet) active dry yeast
  (not instant)

1 cup warm milk (110°F)

4 tablespoons (1/2 stick) unsalted butter, melted and cooled a bit

3 large egg yolks

3 1/2 cups pastry flour

2 tablespoons sugar

1 1/2 teaspoons kosher salt

8 cups canola oil, for frying

2 cups sugar, for rolling

2 cups seedless jelly of your choice

Make the Yeast Sponge:

In a small bowl, dissolve the yeast in the warm water and mix in the flour until fully combined. Cover with a towel and leave in a warm place until bubbly and doubled in size, about 2 hours.

Make the Donuts:

In a small bowl, dissolve the yeast in the warm milk.

Transfer the yeast sponge to the bowl of an electric mixer fitted with a dough hook attachment. With the mixer running on low, add the milk-yeast mixture, the butter, and the egg yolks.

In a separate bowl, whisk together the pastry flour, sugar, and salt. Add these dry ingredients to the wet in three batches. Knead on medium speed until the dough is pulling away from the sides of the bowl and forming a ball around the dough hook, about 3 minutes.

Transfer the dough to a large oiled bowl. Cover with a towel and place in the fridge to proof for 12 to 16 hours.

Turn out the dough onto a floured surface and roll it to about 1/2 inch thick. Cut with whatever circle cutter size you prefer — I made 30 mini (2-inch) donuts and 4 big (3 1/2-inch) donuts. You can reroll the scraps once; just bring the dough back into a ball and let it rest for 5 minutes or so.

After punching out the donuts, lay them on a piece of oiled parchment and let them rise in a warm place for 30 minutes.

When you're ready to fry, heat the canola oil in a Dutch oven or heavy-bottomed large pot over medium-high heat until it reaches 350°F. Fry the donuts in batches, making sure you keep the temperature at or around 350°F. Change the oil if it gets too filled with dough debris. My 2-inch donuts were done after 1 minute per side and my 3 1/2-inch donuts were done after 2 1/2 minutes per side.

Toss the fried donuts in a bowl of sugar while they are still warm, poke a hole in them with a skewer or a small knife, load up a pastry bag with jelly, and fill those suckers up.

The Dog Stars
WHOLE ROASTED TROUT

I have never been a fan of postapocalyptic literature. The world, to me, is terrifying and confusing enough on a daily basis without all of the fire and brimstone, collapsing buildings, and dwindling food supplies. In college I tried reading Cormac McCarthy's *The Road* because I was smitten with a guy who said it was his favorite book. "*The Road,*" he told me, "is full of adventure and friendship and humor. It changed my entire view of what it means to be a man." We were eating comically large burgers at Paul's on St. Mark's Place and talking, in the earnest and embarrassing way that college students do, about books that we felt *defined* us. I remember thinking vaguely, as he wiped melted cheese from his mouth, that I would be a bit mortified if anyone was eavesdropping on our conversation.

When we had finished our burgers I walked over to the bookstore. *The Road* had just come out a few months earlier and was still prominently displayed in the front window of the shop. The man at the counter shuddered while ringing it up — "You're brave for this one, girly," he told me, pushing it into my hands so eagerly it was as if the cover was burning his. I made it through about twenty pages on my subway ride home and by the time I walked in my front door and looked in the mirror my face was ashen and my knees felt like Jell-O. After fifty pages I was in a cold sweat and had to tuck the book into a drawer in the other room before trying to fall asleep. Adventure? Friendship? Humor? Had he even read this book? I felt betrayed.

A few days later I was invited to his apartment for dinner. I was building up the nerve to tell him that I couldn't make it past fifty pages of his favorite book when I noticed a stack of multiple editions of Jack Kerouac's *On the Road* on his coffee table. Opening one up I saw that it was absolutely covered with underlines and stars, notes and exclamations, in boyish handwriting — it looked not unlike all of my favorite books. It suddenly occurred to me that I had tortured myself with *The Road* for no reason at all. This guy was no Cormac McCarthy fan. And while I can chalk up forgetting the name of your favorite novel to first-date jitters, allowing Jack Kerouac to define for you what it means to be a man is, for me, an issue. That dinner was our last.

I gave my unfinished copy of *The Road* to my neighbor across the hall and didn't touch another postapocalyptic novel until a friend gave me a copy of Peter Heller's *The Dog Stars* a couple of months ago. She, and many of the reviews I read, described it as "*The Road* but with hope," which is probably why it took me so long to pick it up — I was terrified of reading anything remotely like *The Road.* When I finally did crack it open, though, I was not sorry at all.

In sparse and heartrendingly beautiful prose, Heller tells the story of a man named Hig who has lost everything to a superflu that wiped out ninety percent of the human race. He lives in the hangar of an abandoned airport with his dog, Jasper, and a man named Bangley who seems to enjoy the cruelty and violence that surviving in a postapocalyptic world allows him to enact. What sets *The Dog Stars* apart from other novels of its kind is Hig himself. *The Dog Stars* is more about what it means to be human than about what happens when "civilized" society crumbles.

What really set this novel apart for me, though, was the food. Normally in novels of this kind there is very little (if any) food, and what's there is seldom appetizing. The food in *The Dog Stars,* on the other hand, is mouthwatering. Hig plants beans, tomatoes, and potatoes, eats venison heart, cooks catfish with dandelion salad and basil, makes wild strawberry, black raspberry, and mint tea from a jar of summer flowers, eats shepherd's pie dripping with butter, and drinks pitcher after pitcher of cold milk. The most powerful, most prevalent food scenes in the book, though, are ones involving fishing — trout fishing specifically.

By the third sentence of the novel Hig has already told us that before the superflu, his favorite pastime had been to fish for trout. Once it hit, Hig watched as most of the animals on earth disappeared, but he never cried, he says, "until the last trout swam upriver looking for maybe cooler water." The most poignant memories Hig has of his wife, Melissa, are of her fishing for trout with him — how "she didn't have the distance and accuracy in her cast but she could think more like a trout than probably anyone alive." Hig fishes before disaster strikes, he fishes when the flu hits; when Melissa dies, he fishes with Jasper in the mountains, salts his catches on flat stones, and "pull[s] out the skeleton from the tail up, unzipping the bones."

In the summertime when I was growing up, my dad would wake me while it was still dark outside and we would go fishing for sea bass in the cold black of the Atlantic Ocean. It was thrilling, sneaking around the bedroom trying to get dressed as quietly as possible while my sisters slept. My dad waited in the kitchen, where the smell of newspapers and coffee and aftershave hung heavy, the nighttime sounds of crickets still creaking through the window screens.

After fishing we always went to a breakfast place called Arno's and ordered enormous stacks of buttermilk pancakes and tiny griddles of corned beef hash. At first this was what I looked forward to most about these fishing excursions. The casting and the waiting and the shivering were, in the beginning, just a means to an end, but eventually I grew to love the pre-pancake ritual, too. I never became a great fisherwoman, but I learned volumes about patience and silence.

One morning I caught a horseshoe crab by accident and reeled it in as it scrambled and scratched against my hook. I had only ever seen dried-up pieces of them on the shore, so catching one in all of its prehistoric glory gave me pause. It was as if the world suddenly threw back its hood and revealed just how tremendously old and sturdy it was and how easily it would continue to thrive once we are, all of us, gone.

THE DOG STARS

Whole Roasted Trout
Serves 3 to 4

1 (2-pound) rainbow trout, gutted and scaled
Kosher salt
2 thyme sprigs
2 garlic cloves, halved
1/2 lemon, sliced into thin rounds
1 tablespoon unsalted butter, cut into 4 pieces
2 tablespoons olive oil
Coarsely ground black pepper
1 cup dry white wine

Preheat the oven to 450°F.

Rinse the fish and pat it dry. Salt the inside of the fish well and place it in a shallow baking dish. Stuff the cavity with the thyme, garlic, lemon slices, and butter. Rub the outside of the fish with the olive oil and sprinkle with salt and pepper. Tie the fish in two places with kitchen twine to hold the herbs and lemon in place. Add the white wine to the baking dish and cover with aluminum foil.

Roast for 15 minutes. Remove the foil and roast for 7 to 10 more minutes. The meat will release from the bones and you should be able to "unzip" the fish and enjoy the meat easily.

THE HOURS
BIRTHDAY CAKE

Early on in my days as a baker, I was given the last-minute task of creating a birthday cake for a high-paying regular customer. My boss was out sick, so the job fell to me, a Duncan Hines cake mix enthusiast with zero formal pastry training and caffeine-shaky hands. In tears, I called my older sister, a professional cake decorator, from the restaurant's trash closet, pleading with her to leave work and come help me. The best she could do was send me a quick email with some pointers and tricks, which I clung to like the last life vest on a sinking ship, reading and rereading it until I had it memorized.

In the end, the cake was slightly crooked and covered in so many layers of vanilla buttercream my teeth ache to think about it. I dodged the task of writing in icing by making a banner out of brown paper and letter stamps and hid the cake's frosting imperfections by dumping a layer of white nonpareils all over it. It looked homemade in a way that I hoped would be charming in the restaurant's dim lighting. The customer was overjoyed, but my chef was horrified, and I was never allowed near a birthday cake order at that restaurant again.

In cooking and baking there is almost always a discrepancy between what you imagine you are capable of creating and what, in the end, comes out of your oven. Sometimes this is a beautiful thing — that soufflé that you were certain would sink? It miraculously rose like a phoenix from the rye-toast ashes of your 1970s Mark Royal oven. And that leg of lamb you were sure you had oversalted? It was a revelation! But sometimes you are *certain* that what you are going to create will be a masterpiece, a dish so wondrous that it will communicate exactly how much you love the person you made it for and, probably because of these outsized expectations and grandiose plans, you are disappointed with the outcome. For me, this is never truer than with birthday cakes, which come with a tremendous amount of "This is my special day" pressure attached to them.

Ever since I read Michael Cunningham's novel *The Hours* in my senior year of high school, it is impossible for me to bake a birthday cake without thinking of poor Laura Brown. Laura, a housewife in suburban Los Angeles in the late 1940s, is determined to create the perfect birthday cake for her husband, Dan — a cake that is as "glossy and resplendent as any photograph in any magazine," one that will "speak of bounty and delight the way a good house speaks of comfort and safety."

Much like the famous *boeuf en daube* scene in Virginia Woolf's *To the Lighthouse*, in which Mrs. Ramsay stresses and panics over the necessity of the stew being absolutely perfect so that all of her guests will know that *she* is perfect, Laura's cake is so much more than just a cake. In Laura's mind, if she can create the perfect cake, it is proof that she can be the perfect wife and mother, that she can be satisfied and fulfilled

with her life, and that she can be happy —
which she knows she should be and is not.

This is much too much pressure to place
on a birthday cake and on herself and it
turns out, of course, to be "less than she
hoped it would be." There are crumbs
caught in the icing and the "n" in "Dan" is
squished from landing too close to the frosting roses. The whole thing "feels small, not
just in the physical sense but as an entity."
The breaking point comes when Laura's
neighbor Kitty comes over for coffee and
calls Laura's cake "cute," sending her into a
spiral of agonizing shame over having
"produced something cute, when she had
hoped (it's embarrassing but true) to produce something of beauty." It would have
been better, she thinks, never to have tried
at all, to have been careless and cavalier and
declare herself "hopeless at such projects"
than to have been caught trying, and failing. Laura throws the cake in the trash and
starts over.

She feels better about the second cake,
and despite Laura's brief, hot rage at the
sight of her husband spraying a sheen of
spittle across her creation when he blows
out the candles her cake is a resounding
success. Dan declares it "perfect," and
Laura feels whole for the first time in days.

The secret is, of course, that even the crumbliest, ugliest homemade cake will always, always mean more than the glossiest and sleekest store-bought cake. We know this by now, don't we? In my life, the cakes that have brought me to tears, that have filled me with such gratitude and love that I feel swollen and glowing, were never beautiful. My favorite cake to make for my friends is a confetti cake, just like the from-a-mix kind you used to beg your parents for every year. It is nostalgic and delicious, and regardless of your cake-decorating skills, it will look beautiful under all those sprinkles.

THE HOURS

Birthday Cake

This recipe produces a triple-layer yellow cake. If you want your cake to be white, substitute 1 cup vegetable shortening for the butter. Sweet butter extract can be purchased online or at specialty baking stores. It gives your cake that boxed-cake taste — in a good, nostalgic way. If you can't find it or don't want to use it, substitute 1 1/2 teaspoons pure vanilla extract plus 1/2 teaspoon pure almond extract.

Serves 8 to 10

1 cup (2 sticks) unsalted butter, at room temperature

1 1/2 cups sugar

2 teaspoons sweet butter extract

3 large eggs, separated (place whites in the refrigerator until ready to use)

2 1/4 cups cake flour

3 1/2 teaspoons baking powder

1 teaspoon kosher salt, plus 1 additional pinch for whipping egg whites

1 1/4 cups buttermilk

3 1/2 cups rainbow sprinkles (the waxy kind used for ice cream toppings, not shiny sugar crystals, which will melt and disappear during cooking) or nonpareils

Vanilla Buttercream Frosting (recipe follows)

Preheat the oven to 350°F. Line the bottom of three 8-inch cake pans with parchment paper. Grease the parchment and sides of each pan and dust the pans with flour, tapping out the excess.

In the bowl of an electric mixer fitted with a paddle attachment, beat the butter until smooth. Add the sugar and butter extract and beat until fluffy, about 3 minutes. Beat the egg yolks into the butter mixture, one at a time.

In a bowl, sift together the flour, baking

powder, and salt and add to the butter mixture in three batches, alternating with the buttermilk. Beat until smooth.

Transfer the batter to a large bowl and wash and dry the bowl of the electric mixer. Add the chilled egg whites and a pinch of salt to the mixer bowl and attach the whisk attachment. Whip the whites at medium-high speed until they hold stiff (but not dry) peaks. This can also be done in a large bowl with an electric hand mixer, or with some biceps strength and a whisk.

Using a spatula, gently fold the stiff egg whites into the batter until they are all mixed in. Quickly fold 1 1/2 cups of the sprinkles into the batter (the colors will run quickly, so don't overmix). Divide the batter evenly among the three prepared cake pans and bake until a toothpick inserted into the center comes out clean, about 35 minutes. Let the cakes cool in their pans on a cooling rack for a bit before turning them out onto the cooling rack to cool completely.

Place the first cooled cake layer on a cake stand and spread the top with roughly 1/2 cup of frosting, smoothing until the frosting is in an even layer. Place the second cake on top and repeat. Do this again with the third layer and cover the outside of all three layers with a thin layer of icing. Place the cake in the refrigerator and allow the messy crumb layer of icing to set until it's completely hardened, 30 to 40 minutes.

Once the crumb coating has set, take the cake out of the refrigerator and frost it with the remaining frosting. Cover in the remaining 2 cups sprinkles and present to the birthday boy or girl.

Vanilla Buttercream Frosting
Makes about 6 cups

1 cup (2 sticks) unsalted butter, at room
    temperature
1/2 cup whole milk
2 teaspoons pure vanilla extract (clear, if
    you can find it, to keep the frosting white)
8 cups confectioners' sugar, sifted
1/4 teaspoon kosher salt

In the bowl of an electric mixer fitted with a paddle attachment, combine the butter, milk, vanilla, 4 cups of the confectioners' sugar, and the salt and beat on medium speed for 3 minutes. Slowly add the remaining sugar, 1/2 cup at a time, beating well after each addition. Once it is all incorporated, increase the mixer speed to high and beat for 1 more minute.

"GOODBYE TO ALL THAT"

GRILLED PEACHES WITH
HOMEMADE RICOTTA

Four years ago, after a string of terrible jobs and a long winter without heat, I started to wonder if New York was the right place for me. A number of my friends had begun to migrate home after college, back to Phoenix and Portland and Oakland — places I had never been and couldn't picture. At night, after serving people coffee all day and making eight dollars in tips, I often found myself staring at photos of my old friends' new lives — sunset hikes through craggy brush-covered mountains, lantern-lit tents on the beach under the stars, homemade chicken coops in the backyards of entire houses that cost less than a New York City studio. They all looked fitter, healthier, happier than I had ever seen them in New York, a kind of celestial glow throbbing around them and emanating out of my computer screen.

So, one night, after a bit too much wine, my friend Willa and I bought two tickets to California. For ten days we adventured from Los Angeles to Santa Rosa to San Francisco, eating the brightest produce I had ever seen, riding two-seater bicycles around the Mission, feeling the sun on our backs. And then those ten days were up, and I arrived home to a rainy and unseasonably cold New York, still smelling like In-N-Out Burger and carrying a backpack full of peaches from the Ferry Building. My first day back I bought sixty dollars' worth of cheese from an old man at the farmers' market because I felt bad for him and cried at a wooden flute rendition of "Chariots of Fire" playing in a nail salon before crawling into bed and wallowing for almost thirty-six hours.

Just when I thought nothing could pull me out of the "Am-I-still-in-love-with-New-York?" pity hole I had buried myself in, I noticed Joan Didion's *Slouching Towards Bethlehem* on my bedside table. I had meant to pack it to read on my trip but had forgotten, and there it sat, still unread and giving off that wonderful new-book smell. I cracked it open and read the first line to the essay "Some Dreamers of the Golden Dream": "This is a story about love and death in the golden land, and begins with the country." For the next four hours, as the light outside my apartment window went from yellow to orange to blue to black, I devoured every essay. By the time I got to "Goodbye to All That" and read the first two paragraphs I was crying like I hadn't cried in years.

Didion's ability to capture perfectly what it is to be young and hopeful and in love with a place — specifically this place, *this* city, that has molded and broken so many — is the reason that "Goodbye to All That" has remained a cult classic forty-eight years after its publication. The essay first appeared in a 1967 edition of the *Saturday Evening Post,* where it was titled "Farewell to the Enchanted City." Didion changed the name to "Goodbye to All That" for its 1968 publication in *Slouching Towards Bethlehem,* perhaps as a nod to Robert Graves's 1929 autobiography of the same name, in which he writes about his "bitter leave-taking of England." Didion's leave-taking is not bitter, but her feelings of grief over leaving the city that she loved "the way you love the first person who ever touches you and you never love anyone quite that way again" are real.

What stuck with me most about the essay wasn't the moment that Didion realized that it was time for her to move on; it was the small moments she shared with this city when it was still so new and beautiful and exciting to her that stood out. Like the day she stood on the corner of Sixty-Second Street and Lexington Avenue eating a peach: "I could taste the peach and feel the soft air blowing from a subway grating on my legs and I could smell lilac and garbage and expensive perfume." It's the tiniest, most innocent moment, but the familiarity of it knocked the wind out of me. Rather than feeling, as Didion did, that it was time to leave New York City, I felt my love of this place renewed.

I pulled myself out of bed. I strapped on my backpack full of California peaches and hopped on my bike, suddenly aware of and immensely grateful for the early springtime smells of Brooklyn — hot concrete, wet mulch, old cigarettes, new grass, deli coffee. I rode to my friend Sam's apartment, a tiny sublet with a clown-car's worth of strange roommates and an enormous roof with a view of Manhattan that made it bearable. We climbed to the roof and split the peaches — which were now bruised and soft — and grilled them on a greasy hibachi.

Our friends came, bringing jelly jars of homemade farmer's cheese, and fresh herbs grown on their fire escape, and bottles of wine pilfered from restaurant jobs. That night I felt vaguely aware that I was only twenty-four, that if Didion was right I still had four more years until I would feel, as she had, that I had "stay[ed] too long at the Fair." I'm here now, in my twenty-eighth year — my tenth in New York — and I'm still waiting.

"GOODBYE TO ALL THAT"

Grilled Peaches with Homemade Ricotta
Makes 6 filled peach halves

3 1/2 cups whole milk
1/2 cup heavy cream
3/4 teaspoon coarse sea salt
3 tablespoons fresh lemon juice
3 ripe peaches, cut in half and pitted
2 tablespoons olive oil, plus more for drizzling
2 teaspoons sugar

Flaky sea salt (such as Maldon), for serving
Coarsely ground black pepper, for serving

Pour the milk, cream, and salt into a large, heavy-bottomed pot and cook over medium-low heat, stirring occasionally, until the temperature reaches 190°F on a candy thermometer. Remove the pot from the heat and stir in the lemon juice. Allow the mixture to sit for 5 to 7 minutes before straining it through a sieve lined with three layers of cheesecloth. Let the cheese drain into a bowl for 1 to 2 hours.

Preheat a grill to medium.

Brush the peaches with the olive oil and dust them lightly with the sugar. Place the peaches, flesh-side down, on the grill and cook until char marks appear, about 2 minutes. Transfer the peach halves to bowls and spoon the fresh ricotta over them. Drizzle the ricotta with olive oil and sprinkle with flaky sea salt and coarse black pepper. Serve immediately.

AMERICAN PASTORAL
HOT CHEESE SANDWICH

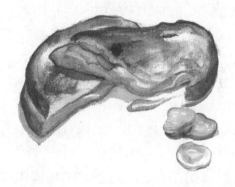

Having served food to the public in one capacity or another for more than a decade, I have encountered my fair share of truly terrible customers. Even years later I can conjure the very worst ones in my mind like it was yesterday, their sour faces and cruel words, their determination to be dissatisfied. There was the hotshot in his expensive suits who always called me "Big Guy" when he came to order his double Americanos. A joke, maybe, but precisely the kind of joke a nineteen-year-old girl who has just packed on the freshman fifteen is not entirely equipped to handle.

There was the woman who always paid for her bagel and coffee with hundreds of pennies, and the man whose vanilla latte was never hot enough, even when the milk was burned. The person I dreaded most, though, was a seven-year-old boy — a tiny ruddy-cheeked terror whose memory still makes me shudder. Every morning, without fail, an enormous production was made about what the little boy would eat for breakfast. Would it be a croissant? No! He hated croissants today. Maybe a bagel? Disgusting! Yogurt, no. Sandwich, no. Muffin, no. His parents cooed and soothed and petted, but the decision was never simple. He stomped and huffed and flailed, whining like a mosquito. In the end, he always got a chocolate chip cookie as big as his face, despite having refused it multiple times, and left looking smug, leaving a long line of frustrated customers in his wake. Even now, my palms sweat to think about him. I was amazed by the power this tiny child had over his parents, over all of us.

When I read Philip Roth's *American Pastoral* a few years ago for my book club, I thought of this little boy the entire time, because his food rebellions reminded me so much of Merry Levov's. For Merry, what she eats and how much she eats is the first thing she is able to control in her life, and she uses her eating habits as a weapon against her parents, whose idyllic, bourgeois American life she detests and seeks to destroy.

Nathan Zuckerman, Roth's favorite pseudo alter ego and the book's narrator, learns of the "tragedies that have befallen" Merry's father, Seymour "The Swede" Levov — the golden god of Newark, New Jersey — from Seymour's brother, Jerry, while at his forty-fifth high school reunion. Jerry tells Nathan that his brother has just died of prostate cancer, after suffering for years in the wake of Merry's terrorist act of bombing the local general store. Jerry launches into a venomous speech about Merry, whom he calls Seymour's "darling fat girl," saying, "It's one thing to get fat . . . but it's another to jump the line and throw a bomb." It seems that these two sentences stick with Nathan, because in his reimagining of Merry's story, her relationship to food is an integral part of her rebellion.

The rest of the novel is Zuckerman's piecing together of the years leading up to Merry's violent act of terror, his attempt to get to the root of how things had gone so terribly wrong for a man who had always done his best to do everything right. Zuckerman is determined to find the cause of Merry's violence, to draw a complete line from her childhood to the day that she blew up the general store, to show us the signs that the Swede missed. To the Swede, who is blinded by his love for Merry, her violence springs from nowhere, completely unexpected. Zuckerman, however, paints her as a little girl who is rebellious from the very start and who wields her power early on by what and how much she eats.

Merry's first act of rebellion is not eating the lunches her mother packs her for school. She hates bologna, detests liverwurst, abhors tuna — the only thing Merry likes is Virginia ham sandwiches with the crusts cut off, and hot soup, which she can't have since she is constantly breaking even the most indestructible of thermoses. Merry throws her lunches away every day, subsisting only on the ice cream she buys with the dime Seymour leaves at the bottom of her lunch bag, and her favorite food — melted cheese sandwiches.

As a teenager, Merry continues to refuse any food served to her at home, but at school and elsewhere gorges on junk food "so that almost overnight she became large, a large, loping, slovenly sixteen-year-old." By gaining weight, and refusing to brush her hair or teeth or wash her face, Merry defies everything that is most important to her beauty-queen mother, and also rejects the American ideal of beauty. Right before Merry plants the bomb she goes to a diner and orders a BLT and a vanilla milkshake — a meal she thinks of as "the ritual sacrament." Merry hates, *detests* America, but she actively consumes it in the most literal way through the foods she chooses to eat — cheeseburgers, processed-cheese sandwiches on white bread, milkshakes, BLTs, pizza, onion rings, root beer floats, and French fries.

When Seymour finds Merry, five years after her terrorist act, she has converted to Jainism, an Indian religion whose followers pledge never to harm any living being. This belief leads Jainites to stringently abstain from eating all animal protein and by-products, and any plants whose cultivation harms any living creature. When Seymour sees her, he is shocked at how thin she is. Her extreme behavior still relies on food as a controlling device, a form of rebellion. Early on it was gluttony, later in her life it was abstinence — two sides of the same coin.

When my book club met to talk about the book I made BLTs and vanilla milkshakes — Merry's "ritual sacrament" — but my heart wasn't quite in it. I couldn't get the melted cheese sandwiches out of my brain. When I was young, my dad used to take my sisters and me to a diner called the Nite Owl near where he grew up, in Fall River, Massachusetts. The diner was a tiny stainless-steel box striped with red enamel and dressed up with neon signs. It sat smack in the middle of a Shell gas station parking lot. Although they offered cheeseburgers and Coney Island–style hot dogs, we went there for one thing and one thing only — a sandwich called the "hot cheese."

This was not a grilled cheese sandwich, it was a buttered, grilled hamburger bun stuffed with melted cheese that had the texture of curds and the tang of a super-sharp cheddar. It was slathered in yellow mustard and piled high with diced raw onions and sweet pickle relish. It was heartburn-inducing heaven, that hot cheese. We washed it down with Autocrat coffee milk and felt the burn of it in our chests all day long. Every time Merry's melted cheese sandwiches were mentioned I thought of those hot cheese sandwiches, their grease-spattered paper collars, their potato bun like the smoothest surface of the moon, a tiny American flag toothpick buried in its craters — American diner food par excellence.

AMERICAN PASTORAL

Hot Cheese Sandwich
Serves 1

1 teaspoon unsalted butter
1 hamburger bun (the cheap kind)
4 ounces very sharp cheddar cheese, cut into thin slices
1 teaspoon French's yellow mustard
1 tablespoon sweet pickle relish
1 tablespoon minced white onion

Preheat the grill or a stovetop grill pan, and the broiler. Line a baking sheet with aluminum foil.

Butter each half of the hamburger bun and grill it, butter-side down, until it's toasted and you can see char marks. Pile the cheddar onto the bottom half of the bun and place it on the lined baking sheet. Put it under the broiler until the cheese is completely melted and bubbly, about 5 minutes. Spread yellow mustard on the top half of the bun, pile the sweet relish and raw onions on top of the cheese, put the whole thing together, and eat your heart out.

EMMA
PERFECT SOFT-BOILED EGG

It took me a long time to come around to Jane Austen's *Emma.* I blame this mostly on the fact that my English teacher played *Clueless* for us before we read the book, a tactic that made most of the girls in my class adore Emma right from the get-go, but it sullied the experience for me. Every time Emma spoke, I heard the whiny Valley Girl drone of Cher Horowitz. Besides that, my friend-crush on Elizabeth Bennet was at that point so deep that I didn't feel I had any room left in my heart for the deeply flawed Emma Woodhouse. She is insensitive and spoiled, irritatingly beautiful and talented, careless and often, well, clueless.

Unexpectedly, it was butchery that brought me back to *Emma*. Say what you will about Emma Woodhouse, but that young lady knows her way around a pig, which I happen to find endearing. Two entire pages of the novel center on what to do with a newly killed porker from the Woodhouse property. Emma's father, ever the worrier, is overwhelmed by the task of sending pork to a neighbor, but Emma puts him at ease, telling him confidently, "My dear papa, I sent the whole hind-quarter. I knew you would wish it. There will be the leg to be salted, you know, which is so very nice, and the loin to be dressed directly in any manner they like."

Last spring, while I was attempting to make a traditional English country ham at the butcher shop, this scene popped into my head, and that night I picked up *Emma* again for the first time since high school. My reading experience the second time around was entirely different from the first, perhaps because I've gotten even more obsessive about literary food scenes in my old age. Of all of Austen's novels, *Emma* gives readers the clearest glimpse into the unglamorous, everyday tasks of running a household in the early 1800s, a time when even a woman as privileged as Emma Woodhouse would have been knowledgeable about the raising, killing, and preserving of her family's livestock.

In her letters, Austen herself writes often of the livestock kept at Steventon, where she lived with her family. In one letter she tells her sister, Cassandra, about providing a neighbor with pork from their land, much as Emma and her father do in the novel, saying, "My father furnishes him with a pig from Cheesedown; it is already killed and cut up, but it is not to weigh more than a stone; the season is far too advanced to get him a larger one. My mother means to pay herself for the salt and the trouble of ordering it to be cured by the spareribs, the souse, and the lard." Even if the Austen women aren't in the kitchen stirring the pots and baking the bread, each member of the Austen family is involved at some level in the keeping and processing of livestock and produce, knowledge that wouldn't have been at all uncommon at the time or unladylike to discuss in letters.

Mr. Woodhouse, Emma's hypochondriac father, whose "own stomach [can] bear nothing rich," is the catalyst for most of the food talk in the novel. He is constantly trying to convince people to eat something other than what they are eating, to eat less, or to eat nothing at all. At Mrs. Weston's wedding he anxiously tries to dissuade the guests from eating the wedding cake, worried that it "might certainly disagree with many — perhaps with most people, if not taken moderately." In another scene, Emma serves minced chicken and scalloped oysters to her dinner guests, while her father, whose "feelings were in sad warfare" on such occasions, recommends that they all eat gruel, as he is, for their health.

When no one pays attention to him, he tries to push one guest in another gustatory direction, saying: "Mrs. Bates, let me propose your venturing on one of these eggs. An egg boiled very soft is not unwholesome. Serle understands boiling an egg better than any body. I would not recommend an egg boiled by any body else; but you need not be afraid, they are very small, you see — one of our small eggs will not hurt you." I remember thinking that this line was particularly funny my first time reading it — the idea that someone could understand boiling an egg better than anybody else seemed especially ridiculous. What is there to understand about the world's simplest culinary task? I didn't know then what I know now, which is that the method of perfectly soft-boiling an egg is (and apparently always has been) a contentious issue.

The first thing I was ever asked to do when I went for a job trial at a restaurant was soft-boil an egg. The restaurant was fancy — much fancier than I had any business walking into with only home cooking skills in my back pocket — and I was shocked and ecstatic that this was my first test. I had hard-boiled a million eggs in my life, especially during those lean-wallet college days, and I had my method down pat. All I would have to do is cut that time down by maybe a minute or two and I would have a perfectly soft-boiled egg, right?

The chef handed me an egg; it was ice cold, smaller than I was used to, soft blue, and covered in sandpapery speckles. "This just came out of the hen about an hour ago," he told me without seeming very impressed about it, and walked out of the kitchen. I did what I knew how to do. I put the egg in a small saucepan, I covered it in cold water, I brought it up to a boil and kept it there for five minutes — two minutes less than I would have for a hard-boiled egg. Afterward, I dunked it in ice water and kept it there until I felt confident that it was cool enough to peel and carried it carefully to the office, rolling and clinking against the white china bowl with each step.

Without glancing at it the chef grabbed the egg and gently tapped it against the corner of his desk, then he turned it over and rolled it along his desk, pressing it down gently with the heel of his flat, meaty palm. I felt oddly sorry for the egg then, its speckled blue shell crackling so violently in that clean and silent office. He turned the egg in his cupped hand and, with a raw, chewed-up fingernail, attempted to peel it. The first blue shard tore away and with it came a chunk of white so enormous that I could see the bright orange yolk within, bulging and straining to ooze out. "Nope," he said, and I took that as my cue to gather my things and leave.

Up until that day, boiling an egg was, in my mind, something done carelessly, out of desperation when my stomach was grumbling and there was nothing in my fridge. In the world of professional cooking, though, it's as telling a sign of your kitchen skills as how evenly diced and unbruised your chives are. Any chef you ask will have her own precise method of soft-boiling an egg, and believe me, it will be the *only* and the *best* way. It turns out that Mr. Woodhouse was right, there are a million things to understand when it comes to perfectly soft-boiling an egg. The temperature of the egg before going into the water has to be considered, as does the age of the egg (the chef giving me an hour-old, very cold egg already put two strikes against me, which, in hindsight, was certainly part of the test). Weight, time, pot size, water amount — let's stop here before this sounds impossible, because, really, it's very easy. My favorite soft-boiled egg is a six-minute egg — it's as simple as that.

EMMA

Perfect Soft-Boiled Egg
Serves 2

1 tablespoon kosher salt, plus more for seasoning
2 large eggs, at room temperature (the older the better, in terms of ease of peeling)
Cracked black pepper

Pour 3 inches of water into a 2-quart saucepan and add the salt. Cover and heat over medium-high heat.

While the water is coming up to a boil, prepare an ice bath by filling a small bowl with ice cubes and cold water, and set it aside.

Hold each egg firmly and, using a thumb-tack or a needle, carefully prick a small hole in the bottom of the egg (it's easier than it sounds!).

Once the water has come to a rolling boil, gently lower the eggs into the boiling water using a slotted spoon, and immediately set a timer for 6 minutes.

After 6 minutes, remove the eggs from the water with the slotted spoon and submerge them in the ice bath until they are cooled, about 5 minutes. Once they are cooled, peel them under cold running water.

Split them in half and season them with salt and black pepper to taste.

"THE SYSTEM OF DOCTOR TARR & PROFESSOR FETHER"

GOAT CHEESE PUMPKIN PIE

I've been a fan of Edgar Allan Poe for as long as I can remember, but the lack of food in his stories always frustrated me, mostly because I suspected that he would write about it beautifully. One of his lesser-known stories, "The System of Doctor Tarr and Professor Fether," proved my suspicion to be correct. It is one of the only stories in which Poe writes in detail about what his characters are eating, and it is every bit as good as I always dreamed it would be. (Most likely this is also why it is one of my favorites.)

The story, which takes place in the mid-nineteenth century, details the trip of an unnamed narrator to an asylum in France, where a revolutionary new method for treating mental illness, called "the soothing system," is being practiced on the patients. After taking a tour of the asylum, the narrator is invited to dinner, where things begin to take an odd turn.

The narrator is led into the dining room, where "the table was superbly set out. It was loaded with plate, and more than loaded with delicacies." Rather than being impressed, however, the narrator is nauseated, calling the display "absolutely barbaric," noting that "there were meats enough to have feasted the Anakim" and saying, "Never, in all my life, had I witnessed so lavish, so wasteful an expenditure of the good things of life." There is "veal à la Menehoult" and "cauliflowers in velouté sauce" paired with glasses of "clos de Vougeot." There is French-style rabbit, and the centerpiece is "a small calf roasted whole, and set upon its knees, with an apple in its mouth, as is the English fashion of dressing a hare." The narrator, upon seeing the calf being carried over by three waiters, is horrified, and mistakes it for the "monstrum horrendum, informe, ingens, cui lumen ademptum" — *The Aeneid*'s "immense, misshapen, marvelous monster whose eye is out." Something is truly not right here.

As far as food goes, though, the best of Poe is yet to come. The doctors start discussing their patients, many of whom are convinced that they are different types of food. There is the patient "who very pertinaciously maintained himself to be a Cordova cheese, and went about, with a knife in his hand, soliciting his friends to try a small slice from the middle of his leg," as well as "the man who took himself for a bottle of champagne, and always went off with a pop and a fizz." Lastly, there is "Jules Desoulieres, who was a very singular genius, indeed, and went mad with the idea that he was a pumpkin. He persecuted the cook to make him up into pies — a thing which the cook indignantly refused to do." The speaker then adds that she is "by no means sure that a pumpkin pie à la Desoulieres would not have been very capital eating indeed!"

To me, this dinner party sounds like a whole lot of weird fun, but the narrator feels otherwise. He becomes progressively more uncomfortable and suspicious when his host tells him that they are no longer using the revolutionary new soothing system, but a much more rigorous and severe treatment developed by a Doctor Tarr and a Professor Fether. The host explains that they had to stop using the soothing system when the patients, having been given too much freedom, one day turned on their doctors and nurses, locking them up as mental patients and replacing them as staff for over a month. At that moment, a great ruckus erupts, and what do you know? The real doctors and nurses burst into the dining room, exposing the narrator's hosts as the actual mental patients!

As slapstick and silly as the story is, there is genuine fear behind Poe's tale. The nineteenth century was a time of major reform in asylums and the rights of the mentally ill. Only four years before this story was written, Dorothea Dix stood in front of the Massachusetts legislature, telling them that the sick and insane were being "confined in this Commonwealth in cages, closets, cellars, stalls, pens! Chained, naked, beaten with rods, and lashed into obedience." She begged for reform, and slowly it came. That same year, Dr. John Galt opened the first publicly supported mental institution in the United States, where he aimed to treat patients with talk therapy and pharmaceutical drugs rather than simply confining and neglecting them.

At the same time, the public was uneasy over the growing number of acquittals in court cases involving violent crimes where the perpetrator was deemed mentally insane. Anger that the mentally ill were not being held accountable for their crimes was rising, as was the fear that every criminal would feign insanity in order to avoid jail time. Isn't it a relief that we've gotten all of this completely under control in the last two centuries?

Ever since I read this story years ago, I've dreamed about combining two of those mental patients into a single pie, the Cordova cheese and the pumpkin. Cordova cheeses are generally soft goat's or sheep's milk cheeses, often cured in a vegetable ash rind. I imagined mixing this into a pumpkin pie to make a slightly more savory version of the Thanksgiving classic that I've never loved. Here it is: half pumpkin pie, half cheesecake, with a slightly salty almond-rosemary crust that is buttery and sweet but serious. Plus, now you don't even have to stress about your pumpkin pie getting those annoying ugly cracks in the top that make you feel like a giant failure (or is that just me?). Just throw it in the fridge overnight and it's perfectly smooth and ready to go the next day.

"THE SYSTEM OF DOCTOR TARR AND PROFESSOR FETHER"

Goat Cheese Pumpkin Pie
Serves 8

Almond-Rosemary Crust
2 (5.25-ounce) packages Anna's Almond Thins (or any similarly thin almond cookie)
2 tablespoons chopped fresh rosemary
1 teaspoon kosher salt
10 tablespoons (1 1/4 sticks) unsalted butter, melted and cooled a bit

Goat Cheese–Pumpkin Filling
1 (15-ounce) can pumpkin puree (not pumpkin pie filling)
8 ounces soft goat cheese, at room temperature
4 ounces cream cheese, at room temperature
5 tablespoons unsalted butter, melted and cooled a bit
1 1/2 cups confectioners' sugar, sifted

1 1/2 teaspoons pumpkin pie spice
1/2 teaspoon kosher salt

Make the Crust:
Preheat the oven to 350°F.

Pulse the cookies, rosemary, and salt in a food processor until combined. With the processor running, slowly drizzle in the melted butter and run until well combined. The dough should hold together when pinched.

Press the dough firmly into a 10-inch round by 2-inch deep tart pan with a removable bottom. Place a cookie sheet on the bottom rack of the oven to catch any butter that leaks out and bake the crust for 15 minutes. When the crust is cool enough to touch but still warm enough to be pliable, fix any imperfections and set it aside to cool.

Make the Filling:
Combine all of the ingredients in a bowl and puree with a handheld blender (or use a countertop blender) until very smooth; it takes a good amount of whipping at high speed to get all the clumps out. Scoop into the cooled, baked piecrust and smooth the top. Cover and refrigerate for at least 6

hours, or preferably overnight, before serving.

In Cold Blood

CHERRY PIE

When it comes to pie I am an equal-opportunity eater — unless sour cherries are involved. Sour cherry pie wins, every time. When I was a kid I was a huge fan of the individual-size Hostess cherry pies that came in those waxy white wrappers. They were filled with thick, cherry-flavored goop and studded with pieces of . . . cherry? I'm not sure if they were actually cherries or some distant, factory-produced Frankenstein cousin, but they certainly did the trick for me at the time. I used to walk to Fells Market almost every day after school to get one, washing it down with a Cherry Coke on my walk home. Until I was in my late teens I thought that was what cherry pie tasted like, so when I had an actual, homemade sour cherry pie for the first time, it was an absolute revelation.

Ever since reading Truman Capote's *In Cold Blood* a few years ago, I never eat or make a cherry pie without thinking of Nancy Clutter. Her final act as the most wholesome and blameless woman on earth is teaching her teenage neighbor, Jolene Katz, how to make the perfect cherry pie — her blue-ribbon winner with its "oven-hot cherries simmering under the crisp lattice crust."

After the book was published, a writer for *Best Life* magazine dug up Nancy Clutter's actual cherry pie recipe, which I was *so* excited about, until I found out that dear Nancy used frozen premade piecrust and frozen cherries in her version. Frozen cherries I can abide, because cherries are in season for only a short time, but a premade crust won't do. These days, I spend a good deal of time at the Meat Hook reconstituting rendered lard into biscuits and cookies. When early summer comes around and berries start popping up in the markets, I usually focus my lard reconstituting on piecrusts so that our customers can enjoy the season properly — that is, with a freshly made piecrust that contains both butter and real lard. What is real lard? you ask. *Real* lard, the very best lard for baking, comes from pigs.

On Tuesdays at the shop we get our pigs delivered — usually between four and eight of them. No matter how many times I've completed the ritual of the delivery — cleaning off the tables, walking out to the truck, ducking under the weight of the pig and carrying it inside, laying it on the table, and breaking it down into its primals — I am always amazed by how quickly and smoothly and quietly it all happens.

Once the pigs are on the table, the first step in breaking them down is removing the kidney fat — or "leaf lard" — that lies in a smooth, white layer over the pig's abdomen. It comes off without a knife in three or four clean, satisfying yanks. Once it's off we grind it and render it and it becomes the silky, odorless lard of your baking dreams. This stuff is truly magical; it is precisely what Crisco is attempting to mimic with its vegetable shortening, but in my opinion it does an infinitely better job, in terms of both flavor and texture.

I like to think that Capote — who spent his early years living with his aunts, the Faulks, on a farm in Monroeville, Alabama, where they raised chickens and turkeys and smoked hogs in their smokehouse — would have turned up his nose at a premade piecrust. Living off the land that surrounded them, the Faulks ate well. Breakfast was the most important meal of the day there, and, according to Gerald Clarke's biography of Capote, would include "an almost excessive display of the land's bounty" — pork chops and collard greens, cornbread, black-eyed peas, ham and eggs, catfish, squirrel, grits and gravy, raw milk, pound cake with homemade preserves, and coffee made with chicory. His favorite aunt, Sook, combed the woods for pecans to put in her Christmas fruitcakes, and foraged for roots and herbs with which she made medicinal teas. Having spent his childhood surrounded by this kind of farm-to-table plentitude, Capote would have loved this pie.

Cherry Pie

If you are a vegetarian or otherwise anti-lard, you can substitute vegetable shortening or butter (but don't use the hydrogenated lard sold in supermarkets). And if you can find only sweet cherries instead of sour, you'll need to increase the amount of lemon juice to 3 or 4 teaspoons.

Serves 8

Crust
2 1/2 cups all-purpose flour
3 tablespoons sugar
1 teaspoon kosher salt
12 tablespoons (1 1/2 sticks) unsalted butter, cut into 1/4-inch cubes and frozen
1/2 cup rendered leaf lard, cut into 6 pieces and frozen
1/4 cup ice-cold water
1/4 cup chilled vodka
1 large egg
1 tablespoon cream

Filling
3/4 cup sugar
1/4 cup cornstarch
1/4 teaspoon kosher salt

2 pounds sour cherries, pitted and halved
1 teaspoon fresh lemon juice
1/2 teaspoon pure vanilla extract
2 tablespoons unsalted butter, cubed

Make the Crust:

Combine 1 1/2 cups of the flour, 2 tablespoons of the sugar, and the salt in the bowl of a food processor and pulse four times. Add the frozen butter and lard and process until the dough just begins to collect and none of the flour is uncoated, 15 to 20 seconds. Add the remaining 1 cup flour and pulse five times, until pea-sized lumps appear throughout.

Transfer the mixture to a bowl and add the ice-cold water and vodka, using a rubber spatula to gently bring the dough together. It might seem stickier or tackier than you're used to, but all of the vodka will evaporate when baked, so don't fret!

Divide the dough into two even pieces and shape them into balls, being careful not to overhandle. Tightly wrap them in plastic and put them in the refrigerator to chill for at least 2 hours.

After 2 hours, roll out each ball of dough into a 12-inch round on a floured work surface. Stack them on a plate with a layer of greased parchment between them, put them back in the fridge, and preheat the oven to 425°F.

Make the Filling:
Whisk together the sugar, cornstarch, and salt and then add the cherries, lemon juice, and vanilla. Remove the pie dough from the refrigerator and press one round into a 9-inch pie plate. Add the cherry filling, mounding it slightly in the center, and scatter the butter cubes all over the cherries.

Brush the edge of the bottom piecrust with water and gently drape the top crust over the cherries. Fold the excess dough from the bottom crust over the excess dough from the top crust and crimp them together with the tines of a fork.

Cut several vents in the top crust to allow the steam to exit.

Mix the egg and cream together, brush the egg wash all over the crust, and dust with the remaining 1 tablespoon sugar.

Bake for 15 minutes, then reduce the oven temperature to 375°F and continue baking until the crust is golden brown and the filling is bubbling, about 1 hour more. If the crust is getting brown too quickly, tent foil over it and continue to bake.

THE LITTLE FRIEND

PEPPERMINT STICK ICE CREAM

Having read all three of Donna Tartt's novels, I find it impossible to pick which one I like best — they are all so different from one another. *The Secret History* and *The Goldfinch* are both set primarily on the East Coast and have the mystique of dusty intellectualism and old money. This is the kind of atmosphere that most readers came to expect after *The Secret History* was published, and perhaps it's because this expectation was not met, because *The Little*

Friend was so very different, that people were less than enthusiastic about it when it came out in 2002.

Michiko Kakutani, the notoriously harsh *New York Times* book critic, wrote, "At its worst [*The Little Friend*] feels like a Frankenstein of a book, a lumpish collection of mismatched parts," and said that many of the book's action scenes don't seem plausible, but rather like "outtakes from a highly contrived action movie." In my opinion, these observations could be applied to all of Tartt's novels, which are epic and unwieldy — they jump forward and backward in time, and often they ask us to suspend our disbelief, if only for the sake of a truly great story.

In the case of *The Little Friend,* the great story is that of Harriet Dufresnes, a nine-year-old girl growing up in Mississippi, whose older brother, Robin, was found hanging from a tupelo tree in the family's backyard when he was nine (Harriet was just a baby). The book has all of the gothic spookiness that you would expect from a Tartt novel (and then some), but it feels completely different because of its narrator. As much as I loved *The Secret History* and *The Goldfinch,* I did not love or relate to their narrators, Richard and Theo, who seem compulsively driven to make horrible decisions and throw themselves headlong into peril. Harriet is similar in her quest for adventure and danger, but somehow it feels less destructive in the body of a spirited and brave nine-year-old tomboy. Harriet is part Scout Finch, part Caddy Compson, part Harriet Welsch, and yet remains a character all her own.

Because Tartt is so private, the desire to see her in her characters is always there, and with Harriet it's even harder to avoid. Tartt grew up in Mississippi and would have been around nine years old in the early 1970s. Like Harriet, Tartt was an avid reader, and judging by her ability to write fiction, it's safe to assume that she had Harriet's active imagination.

Through Harriet, we are given a glimpse of the kind of hearty Southern food that Tartt was most likely raised on — chicken croquettes and biscuits with Karo corn syrup, banana pudding, coconut cake, corn pudding, mashed potatoes, pound cake, fried chicken. Food is almost always abundant in Southern literature, but in the case of *The Little Friend,* it plays a particularly important role because it shines a light on the ways that grief affects Harriet's family.

After Robin's death, Harriet is often hungry, not only for food, but for love and attention from her nearly catatonic mother, who ignores both her physical and emotional demands. When Harriet's health teacher asks the students to keep a journal of their daily eating habits for class, Harriet is horrified when she realizes how bad her diet is, especially on nights when her mother isn't there to prepare dinner, and she finds herself eating meals like "Popsicles, black olives, toast and butter." Mortified, she tears up the actual list and copies down "a prim series of balanced menus: chicken piccata, summer squash gratin, garden salad, apple compote" from a cookbook called *A Thousand Ways to Please Your Family* that her mother got as a wedding gift.

She envies her friend Hely. "No matter how hot it was," Hely's family "sat down and ate a real supper every night, big, hot, greasy suppers that left the kitchen sweltering: roast beef, lasagne, fried shrimp." The only food we see Harriet's mother eat is peppermint ice cream, which sits in striped gallon tubs in the freezer at all times, and which she seems to be forever trying to push on Harriet as a suitable meal. At one point, Harriet tells her mother point-blank, "I'm starving," to which Harriet's mother responds by offering her the ice cream. Harriet is incensed, and rails at her, saying:

" *'I . . . hate . . . that . . . kind . . . of . . . ice . . . cream.'* . . . How many times had she said it? 'Mother, *I hate peppermint ice cream.'* She felt desperate all of a sudden; didn't anybody ever listen to her? 'I can't stand it! I've never liked it! Nobody's ever liked it but you!' "

In a response as icy cold as the glass of peppermint ice cream in her hand, one that shows just how far detached she is, Harriet's mother looks at her raging daughter and responds simply, "Hmn?"

THE LITTLE FRIEND

Peppermint Stick Ice Cream
Makes 2 1/2 to 3 quarts

3 cups whole milk
3 cups heavy cream
1 teaspoon pure vanilla extract
8 large egg yolks
1 1/2 cups sugar
1/2 teaspoon kosher salt
1 teaspoon pure peppermint extract
1 1/2 cups crushed peppermint candies

Prepare an ice bath by filling the sink or a very large bowl with ice cubes and cold water. Set a large glass or metal bowl over

354

it, and a fine-mesh strainer over the bowl.

In a large, heavy-bottomed pot, combine the milk, cream, and vanilla and heat over medium heat until just before boiling (you will see little bubbles form around the edge of the pan and steam rising from the surface of the liquid).

In a separate large bowl, whisk together the egg yolks, sugar, and salt until fluffy and light yellow.

Transfer some of the scalded milk-cream mixture to a 1-cup glass measuring cup. Slowly pour it into the yolks in a steady stream, whisking constantly. Continue to do this until all of the scalded milk-cream is incorporated into the egg yolks.

Pour the yolk-cream mixture back into the pot and cook over medium-low heat, whisking constantly, until the mixture reaches 170°F. Pour the mixture through the strainer into the bowl over the ice bath, whisk in the peppermint extract, and continue to whisk the base until it cools to room temperature. Cover the bowl and transfer it to the refrigerator to cool completely, at least 8 hours.

When the base is thoroughly cooled, spin it in an ice cream maker according to the manufacturer's instructions. When the ice cream has set, add the crushed peppermint candies and allow it to spin for another minute until they are incorporated throughout. (If your ice cream maker can spin only 1 quart at a time, add 3/4 cup of the candies to 1 quart of base while the ice cream is spinning, then repeat.)

"GIMPEL THE FOOL"

CHALLAH

My grandfather grew up in a Yiddish-speaking household in Dorchester, Massachusetts, with his mother, father, brother, and grandmother. To this day, he still talks about the challah that his grandmother used to make — big braided loaves that she kept warm on the apartment's radiators, filling the whole house with their aroma, and the tiny individual rolls she snuck him and his brother after school. He remembers the challah so vividly that I can taste and smell it whenever he talks about it, but sadly, aside from an armload of everyday phrases and terms of endearment, he doesn't remember how to speak Yiddish.

When I discovered Isaac Bashevis Singer's stories in college, I wished more than anything that I could read them in their original language. Saul Bellow translated "Gimpel the Fool" in 1953, introducing Singer to an American audience for the first time. As good as the translation no doubt is, I suspect that much was lost between the languages. Whenever I ask Papa or my uncle Peter to translate a Yiddish word for me, it takes them full *minutes* to explain — there is always a connection to another word that is reminiscent of something else entirely, which relates to the story of such-and-such — it's beautiful to listen to. If one word takes that long to explain, though, I can only imagine what an impossible task it would be to translate an entire collection of Yiddish stories without losing any meaning along the way.

Regardless of what is lost in translation, I never tire of Singer's writing. Food — specifically bread — is everywhere in *Gimpel the Fool and Other Stories.* In "Abba and His Seven Sons," Pesha, when she baked challah for lunch, "would grasp the first loaf and carry it, hot from the oven, blowing on it all the while and tossing it from hand to hand, to show it to Abba, holding it up, front and back, till he nodded approval." In "The Unseen" a man eats his Rosh Hashanah meal in total darkness — he "blindly dunked a slice of bread in honey, and tasted an apple, a carrot, the head of a carp, and offered a blessing for the first fruit, over a pomegranate."

It was Gimpel the bread baker who first drew me to Singer, and Gimpel whom I thought of all day last week while I made round challahs for Rosh Hashanah. I was lucky enough to be home with my family for the holiday, and my sisters and I spent all day kneading and punching and braiding dough, loaves rising on every radiator, just like in my grandpa's tiny childhood apartment.

"GIMPEL THE FOOL"

Challah

Challah, like most bread, can be tricky. I've tried a million different techniques — letting it rise in the sun, letting it rise in the oven, using honey instead of sugar, increasing the amount of eggs and decreasing the amount of yeast — and they were all good, but not perfect. The trick, as I've learned over and over again with raised doughs, is giving it a cold, slow rise after its first two warm rises. If you're short on time, two warm, fast rises will do just fine, but a cold, slow rise gives the bread a whole new depth of flavor and a texture that's somehow both airy and chewy at once, just as a good challah should be.

Makes 2 loaves

1 1/2 tablespoons active dry yeast
1 tablespoon sugar
1 3/4 cups warm water (110°F)
1/2 cup vegetable oil
5 large eggs
1/2 cup sugar
1 tablespoon fine sea salt
8 cups bread flour
Coarse sea salt, for sprinkling

In the bowl of an electric mixer fitted with a whisk attachment, dissolve the yeast and sugar in the warm water. With the mixer running, whisk the oil into the yeast mixture. Add 4 of the eggs, one at a time, beating well after each addition, then whisk in the sugar and fine sea salt. Remove the whisk attachment and switch to the dough hook.

With the mixer running, slowly add the

flour, about a cup at a time, and mix until the dough just comes together. At this point, turn out the dough onto a floured surface and knead it by hand until it is smooth and elastic, 3 to 5 minutes.

Place the dough in a greased bowl, cover it with a clean towel, and let it rise in a warm place for 1 hour. After an hour it should be about doubled in size. Punch the dough down, cover it again, and let it rise for another 30 to 45 minutes.

After the second rise, refrigerate the covered bowl of dough for 12 to 24 hours.

Line two baking sheets with parchment paper, and lightly grease the parchment. Turn out the dough onto a lightly floured work surface and divide it into two even pieces. Shape the pieces into loaves, and lay one on each lined baking sheet.

Beat the remaining egg in a small bowl and brush it onto the loaves (reserve the remaining egg wash). If you're making round loaves (traditional for Rosh Hashanah), place them in two oven-safe bowls or round cake pans lined with greased parchment paper. Cover and let them rise in a warm place for 1 more hour.

Preheat the oven to 375°F.

Brush the loaves again with the egg wash and sprinkle with the coarse sea salt. Bake until the loaves sound hollow when you tap them in the center, 40 to 60 minutes (the time will vary depending on whether you made round or straight loaves). If you have a thermometer, the internal temperature of the bread should be 190°F. Turn the finished breads out onto a cooling rack. Eat with everything for every meal.

IN THE WOODS
CHOCOLATE-COVERED DIGESTIVE BISCUITS

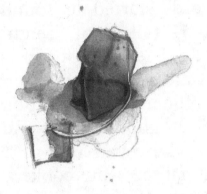

On the Friday after the Boston Marathon bombing in April 2013, I was into my fourth hour of watching the news when I suddenly felt the desperate need to bake. It wasn't the desire to eat something sweet that drove me to it but the calm that measuring, weighing, sifting, creaming, whisking, and waiting always bring me. The sadness and anxiety that I had been feeling since that Monday seemed bottomless, and I baked until I was out of flour, trying to hit bottom so that I could start to come back up.

When you follow news coverage of a major event throughout the day, you sense a language emerging for talking about the story. In the hours before the suspect was taken into custody, news anchors uttered "manhunt" and "shootout" so many times that the words started to sound like nonsense. Others talked of "reading the tea leaves" (code, I learned, for gleaning information by watching the movement of groups of police officers), and emphasized that Boston was a "ghost town," under "virtual lockdown." There was talk of a white hat and a black hat, pressure cookers and IEDs, and the words "Boston Strong" filled my news feeds.

One reporter clung to the word "digest," saying it in one context or another almost twenty times in four hours — "we're still digesting," "hard to digest" — an odd word to grab onto, which is probably why it stood out for me. Funny things happen with appetites and digestion when tragedy and grief are involved. We can't eat, or we overeat, or we crave things we've never craved before or things that we haven't eaten since we were children.

That morning, when all of my butter and

flour and sugar had been baked into cakes and bars, I muted the TV and hid under a blanket with my book — Tana French's *In the Woods.* It was exactly what I needed at that very moment — the well-written murder mystery of my comfort-craving dreams — and I read it for hours, eating nearly an entire grapefruit cake in the meantime, until I finally felt more like myself.

As homicide detectives, Cassie Maddox and Rob Ryan are engulfed by disaster and tragedy, forever grappling with ways to manage their grief. They drink too much, they sleep with the wrong people, they make each other greasy dinners, they pop handfuls of anxiety medication and stay up all night. When all else fails, Cassie eats chocolate digestive biscuits, lots of them. She buys them at the market and hides them in her desk drawer. People bring them to her as bribes and peace offerings and, in an odd twist that I'm not quite sure how to interpret, they are also the last meal of the twelve-year-old girl whose murder is at the heart of the book.

You could certainly argue that the ubiquity of chocolate biscuits in *In the Woods* is due to the fact that the novel is set in Ireland and that Tana French is an Irish writer. According to a *Washington Post* article by

Monica Hesse, digestives have been part of daily life in the UK since their invention in the nineteenth century, and today an estimated fifty-two biscuits are consumed every second. As the name suggests, digestive biscuits were originally created to aid in digestion, the idea being that the coarse bran and heavy amounts of baking soda would settle the stomach and help move things along. This was of particular interest to the Victorians, who were preoccupied with their finicky insides. But, as with the graham cracker, clearly their appeal is far broader than medicinal use.

There is immense comfort in the ritual and the history that is present in every bite of a digestive. During World War II, British soldiers were given two different kinds of biscuits in their rations — two plain and two chocolate — tucked away in their rucksacks with tins of industrial-grade beans and chipped beef. I think about them, scared and young and far from home, and the comfort that these familiar little disks might have brought them in the face of tragedy and disaster and violence.

After hours of being held captive by news that was becoming increasingly repetitive (without much in the way of new information), the comfort that reading and baking had brought me began to wear thin, and I forced myself to leave the house and seek solace elsewhere. I took the train into Union Square and visited my friend Joe at work, and he made me a cocktail with burned rosemary and good gin and it tasted like Christmas and damp earth and made my chest warm. I walked to Chelsea and smelled new books in a tiny bookstore and ate chicken liver so good it immediately brought the color back to my cheeks. I walked from Herald Square to the Battery and then home across the Williamsburg Bridge, and I ate a green tomato like an apple, and it was good and musky and tart. I thought about the city that I'm in, but mostly I thought about the city that I'm from, with its bruised history and mixed-up roads and good, *good* people. The Shabbat sirens wailed in the neighborhoods below me and I cried a little into my tomato as a throng of Hasidic boys rushed past me to make it home before sundown, and I thought about the eighteen Boston Marathons I'd attended, feeling safe and happy and proud, and I took some time to digest it, all of it, everything.

Chocolate-Covered Digestive Biscuits
Makes 1 dozen (3-inch) biscuits

3/4 cup whole-wheat flour
1/4 cup all-purpose flour
1/4 cup wheat bran
1/4 cup plus 1 tablespoon firmly packed
  dark brown sugar
1/2 teaspoon baking powder
1/4 teaspoon baking soda
1/4 teaspoon cream of tartar
1/4 teaspoon kosher salt
4 tablespoons (1/2 stick) unsalted butter,
  browned and chilled to solid
1 tablespoon vegetable shortening, chilled
3 tablespoons heavy cream
1/2 teaspoon pure vanilla extract

Chocolate Glaze
1 cup semisweet chocolate, chopped
2 teaspoons vegetable shortening
Coarse sea salt, for sprinkling

Preheat the oven to 350°F. Line a baking
sheet with parchment paper.

Combine the whole-wheat flour, all-
purpose flour, wheat bran, brown sugar,
baking powder, baking soda, cream of

tartar, and salt in the bowl of a food processor and pulse a few times to get everything evenly mixed. Add the chilled brown butter and vegetable shortening and pulse until the fats are evenly distributed throughout.

With the processor running, slowly add the cream and vanilla.

Turn out the dough onto a clean surface and form it into a ball. The dough will be very crumbly, but don't worry — it will come together. Place the dough between two pieces of parchment paper and roll it to 1/8 inch thick. Cut with a 3-inch circle cutter and place the cookies on the lined baking sheet.

Bake until golden brown and firm, 15 to 20 minutes. Transfer to a wire rack to cool.

To make the glaze, set up a double boiler: Fill a medium saucepan with 2 inches of water and bring it to a simmer over medium heat. Place a heat-safe glass bowl over the pot and add the chocolate and shortening, whisking until smooth. Spread the melted chocolate over the cooled cookies and sprinkle with coarse salt.

Sometimes a Great Notion
BLACKBERRY-HAZELNUT COFFEE CAKE

When I met Emily in my junior year of college, I was so fed up and lonesome and exhausted with New York that I had submitted transfer applications to as many schools as I could think of and was weeks away from leaving and never looking back. Meeting Emily changed the course of my life for a million happy reasons — most importantly, she convinced me to stay in New York and, years later, to create the blog that led to this book.

Four years ago, Emily and her husband,

Ante, and I started a book club. Every time we finished a book they would come over to my apartment and I would cook them a meal from the book so that we could eat while we were discussing. These book club dinners eventually turned into a literary supper club, which then turned into the blog Yummy Books, which was the starting point for this book. At our final book club meeting we discussed Ken Kesey's *Sometimes a Great Notion* and spooned thick stew over tall, buttery biscuits. Emily and Ante told me stories about Oregon, where they both grew up, and promised that it was just as heavenly as Kesey made it sound (and that they wouldn't go back for at least a few more years).

Kesey is best known for *One Flew Over the Cuckoo's Nest,* but in my opinion *Sometimes a Great Notion* is his real masterpiece. The novel takes place in the fictional Oregon town of Wakonda and chronicles the lives of the Stamper family — the only nonunion logging family left in the town. When the unionized loggers go on strike to demand more pay (their hours are being cut thanks to the invention of the chain saw), the Stamper family decides to cross the picket line and single-handedly provide the mills with lumber.

The chaos outside the Stamper household is nothing, however, compared to what is going on inside it. *Sometimes a Great Notion* is a sprawling epic complete with deep-seated brotherly hatred, savage revenge plots, repressed silences, and Oedipal lust. Think Steinbeck's *East of Eden* pumped full of testosterone. There is hardly a bleaker, rawer look into family dysfunction and hardheaded stubbornness.

The only moments of relief from the constant stream of heartache and cold, beating rain come when the Stamper family is gathered around the table. The men wake up in the morning to Viv Stamper's "piles of steaming pancakes." To the logging mill they take paper sacks filled with vinegar-and-mustard-scented deviled eggs, meaty olives, and "creamy brown candy filled with roasted filberts."

At dinnertime they are "elbows and ears over a checkered tablecloth" covered with "deer liver and heart fried in onions, and gravy made from the drippings . . . boiled potatoes and fresh green beans and home-made bread." Viv prepares baked apples so good — stuffed with butter and brown sugar and cinnamon Red Hots — that Leland Stamper, after eating one, goes outside and literally howls at the moon.

Despite having heard countless tales of how magnificent Oregon is over the years, I was still completely blown away when I visited this past summer to attend Emily and Ante's wedding. The people in Oregon are friendly and the coffee is strong. People don't feel the need to tell you what they're really *trying* to do while telling you about their bakery job, and there is always the cleanest kiss of a breeze. I thought of *Sometimes a Great Notion* the whole time I was there, and of my two friends who had no idea what they would become to each other when they sat on my couch four years ago, eating biscuits and bashfully holding hands under a pillow.

Even through the haze of croissants from Ken's Artisan Bakery and Voodoo Doughnuts and Mirror Pond Pale Ale, I couldn't get Viv's "filbert- and blackberry-filled coffee cake" out of my head all week, so the day after the wedding, my feet still sore from dancing (and my head still sore from champagne), I went to the farmers' market and picked up blackberries and some good Oregon hazelnuts and we feasted on the cake until our stomachs hurt. It was a perfect end to what Leland Stamper would have called the "*bless*fullest" week.

Blackberry-Hazelnut Coffee Cake
Serves 8

Blackberry Streusel
1 cup all-purpose flour
1/2 cup firmly packed dark brown sugar
3 teaspoons ground cinnamon
1/2 teaspoon kosher salt
6 tablespoons (3/4 stick) unsalted butter, chilled and cut into pieces
1 1/4 cups roasted unsalted hazelnuts, chopped
1 1/2 cups fresh blackberries

Coffee Cake
12 tablespoons (1 1/2 sticks) unsalted butter, at room temperature
1 1/2 cups granulated sugar
3 large eggs, at room temperature
1 1/4 cups full-fat sour cream
1 1/4 teaspoons pure vanilla extract
2 1/2 cups cake flour (not self-rising)
2 teaspoons baking powder
1/2 teaspoon baking soda
1/2 teaspoon kosher salt

Make the Streusel:

In a large bowl, whisk together the flour, brown sugar, cinnamon, and salt. Add the butter and, using your fingers, pinch the mixture together until it forms a crumble. Add the hazelnuts and knead everything together until big, buttery crumbs form. Toss in the blackberries and mix around to incorporate them throughout. Cover the bowl of streusel and place it in the refrigerator.

Make the Coffee Cake:

Preheat the oven to 350°F. Butter a 10-inch tube pan with a removable bottom.

In the bowl of an electric mixer fitted with a paddle attachment, cream the butter and sugar on medium speed until light and fluffy, about 5 minutes.

Lower the mixer speed and add the eggs, one at a time, beating between each addition to make sure they are well incorporated. Turn off the mixer and scrape down the sides of the bowl. Turn the mixer back on and beat in the sour cream and vanilla.

In a separate bowl, whisk together the flour, baking powder, baking soda, and salt. Add these dry ingredients to the wet and mix just until the batter comes together.

Scrape half of the batter into the tube pan.

Spoon half of the blackberry streusel on top in an even layer. Cover this layer with the rest of the batter and spoon the rest of the streusel on top.

Bake until a toothpick inserted into the center of the cake comes out clean, about 1 hour.

Transfer the pan to a wire rack and cool completely. Once it is completely cooled, turn the cake out, remove the removable bottom, and place the cake streusel-side up on a cake stand or plate.

GONE GIRL
BROWN BUTTER CRÊPES

I love New York in the springtime, because you really get to see how creative New Yorkers are. We can make anything into our own outdoor living space — we sunbathe on the melty tar roofs that our landlords have explicitly banned us from, stretch out and read on rusty fire escapes that haven't been inspected since the 1970s, place seat cushions on cement stoops, and line the sidewalks with lawn chairs. We lay towels over goose poop and sidestep shards of broken glass in public parks, from the Battery to the Brooklyn Bridge, and we ooh and aah with jealousy about people who have actual "backyards," which are almost always private alleyways where we pack ourselves in, shoulder to shoulder, over tiny Weber grills and think, "*This* is living."

In the spring there are long, aimless bike rides and afternoons spent lying in the park, eating yolk-yellow mango slices from the man with the pushcart and sipping from enormous Styrofoam cups filled with Turkey's Nest frozen margaritas (which, let's admit it, are really just yellow Gatorade mixed with tequila), shifting with the position of the sun like houseplants bending and stretching toward the window.

Every year as the days get longer my attention span gets shorter, and I find myself scouring the bookstores for page-turners — pulse-pounding mysteries and thrillers filled with grizzled detectives and sassy, quick-witted heroines — the pulpier the better. In my younger years I held these cravings close to my chest, skittering furtively to those back shelves of the Strand and glancing around to make sure none of my classmates saw me thumbing through a copy of *Scarpetta,* but these days . . . not so much.

Last spring I got that familiar hankering, and with my arms still full of asparagus from the farmers' market, I headed straight to the bookstore. Rather than ducking surreptitiously to those dimly lit back shelves, I asked a store employee for help. Without hesitation, she put her hands on my shoulders and led me straight to *Gone Girl,* her eyes wide and serious as she gave it to me. "You're welcome," she said, and walked away. The next forty-eight hours of my life completely disappeared.

Gone Girl is an easy read only in that it is absolutely impossible to put down. Beyond that, there is nothing easy about this book. Gillian Flynn creates a cast of characters as hard to like as they are to trust. They lie to each other and they lie to us, they pull us to their side only to fill us with disgust a few sentences later — it is a truly exhausting experience.

The novel begins on the morning of Nick and Amy Dunne's fifth wedding anniversary. The couple, who met in New York City, had moved the year before to Nick's hometown of North Carthage, Missouri, to lick their wounds, having both been laid off, and to care for his dying mother and Alzheimer's-stricken father.

The novel opens with Nick lying in bed, listening to the sounds of his wife cooking "something impressive" in the kitchen below him — "probably a crêpe," he imagines. He walks downstairs and finds Amy at the stove, humming the *M*A*S*H* theme song (you know, the "suicide is painless" song — Flynn is a master of the telling minor detail) and making him breakfast. "Amy peered at the crêpe sizzling in the pan and licked something off her wrist. She looked triumphant, wifely. If I took her in my arms, she would smell like berries and powdered sugar."

That evening at the bar he runs, Nick receives a call that his front door is wide open, and he goes home to find Amy missing and the house in complete disarray. As the days tick by and Amy is still missing, the investigation turns on Nick. What follows is one of the darkest accounts of a marriage gone sour that I have ever read.

Aren't you just *starving* for some crêpes right now?

GONE GIRL

Brown Butter Crêpes
Serve these crêpes warm, topped with ricotta, or fruit and maple syrup, or butter, sugar, and lemon zest.

Makes 8 to 10 crêpes

2 large eggs, lightly beaten
1/2 cup whole milk
2 tablespoons honey
1/2 cup all-purpose flour
1/8 teaspoon kosher salt
2 tablespoons unsalted butter, browned and
cooled, plus more for the pan

Beat together the eggs, milk, and honey in the bowl of an electric mixer fitted with a whisk attachment. With the mixer running, add the flour, salt, and browned butter. Cover and refrigerate the batter for 1 hour.

After the batter has chilled, heat a nonstick skillet or crêpe pan over medium heat. Add a little butter (even if you're using a nonstick pan) and ladle 1/4 cup batter in the center of the pan, swirling it around to coat the whole surface evenly. Cook until the surface is set and the edges are golden brown, 1 1/2 to 2 minutes. Flip the crêpe over gently and cook for about 30 more seconds. Repeat with the remaining batter.

The Odyssey
RED WINE–ROSEMARY BREAD

November 2012 was a strange and heavy month. First, there was that stress circus of an election that had me so on edge I was nearly catatonic by the time election night rolled around. In the hours before the results were read I was so overcome with anxiety that I ordered a four-person serving of nachos and found myself unable to eat them. Did you hear me? I said I was *unable to eat nachos.*

Then, there was the explosion of Thanksgiving turkey stress, which seemed to descend upon the butcher shop the very moment people shed their Halloween costumes. For three weeks the phone rang at a constant pace, the voices of people at the other end growing increasingly panicked and close to tears over brining and deep-frying, stuffing and trussing, and the impossibility of finding turkey tenderloin (which, I have to admit, I had no idea was a thing people sold separately).

In the background of all of this was the enormous shadow cast by Hurricane Sandy, which pummeled New York with a vengeance that none of us who had weathered the dud that was Hurricane Irene the year before could have imagined. On the Sunday before the storm hit, the line at the shop spilled out the door and onto the street for hours, until all of the cases were empty. There wasn't a cube of stew beef in sight when we turned the lights off that night, only bins of bones and two bottles of coconut-flavored vodka that had mysteriously appeared on the counter sometime in the afternoon. Everyone was jolly with the prospect of having a couple of days away from work, curling up with a good book or a few movies, cooking and drinking and eating (and eating and eating).

The next morning my coworkers and I

headed back to the shop to prepare it as best we could for the possibility of flooding or loss of electricity. The wind had started to pick up, creating tiny leaf cyclones on the empty streets and in front of the boarded-up storefronts. The sky over the Brooklyn-Queens Expressway was lit up with that doomy, electric, hurricane gray — you know the one I mean? That light that somehow manages to be both the brightest and darkest you've ever seen? The one that makes you think that maybe this hurricane won't just be a cozy, two-day vacation?

By the time I walked back to my apartment later that afternoon I was on the brink of full panic. Consumed by visions of a postapocalyptic Brooklyn, I decided to calm my nerves the best way I know how: by baking bread. I mixed and kneaded and shaped four loaves, and when I finally sat down on the couch I felt somehow calmer knowing that they were all tucked in, rising in the heat of my tiny oven.

Scrolling through storm updates on my computer, I was struck by a photograph in the *New York Daily News* of a man standing in front of a boarded-up bookshop that had been covered in literary quotes about storms. I couldn't quite make out what the quotes said so I started compiling a list in my head of famous literary hurricanes. The best known are probably the storms in Shakespeare's *King Lear* and *The Tempest,* but there are also the epic hurricanes of Daniel Defoe's *Robinson Crusoe* and Chris Adrian's *The Children's Hospital.* Better still are the raging storms in Guy de Maupassant's "The Drunkard" and Kate Chopin's "The Storm."

But no literary character is tossed around by more storms than poor Odysseus. Throughout *The Odyssey* he is constantly being rerouted and delayed by divinely inflicted hurricanes, pushed farther from home and tossed onto islands with lecherous women and hideous beasts. I found my old copy of *The Odyssey,* poured a huge glass of wine, and, with my bread rising in the oven, started to read.

I began to notice how often the words "bread and wine" appear together throughout the text. Homer uses the combination everywhere in *The Odyssey,* and it is always symbolic of being welcomed and safe and home. Bread and wine are ancient staples of comfort and hospitality; they appear in almost every root text, from the Bible to *The Canterbury Tales,* and they always offer relief and solace. For me, they certainly serve that purpose — they are always the first things I reach for in a crisis or offer to a friend having her own. Here, I combine the two comforts into one with delicious results.

THE ODYSSEY

Red Wine–Rosemary Bread

Eat this bread slathered with salted butter and wash it down with more wine.

Makes 1 loaf

3 cups bread flour
2 tablespoons finely chopped fresh rosemary
1 1/2 teaspoons kosher salt
1 teaspoon freshly cracked black pepper
1/2 teaspoon active dry yeast
1/4 cup dry red wine, warmed slightly
1 1/4 cups warm water (110°F)

Sift together the flour, rosemary, salt, and pepper in a large bowl. Dissolve the yeast in the warm wine, add the water to the wine, and pour all of the liquid into the dry ingredients. Mix the dough until it forms a very shaggy ball. Cover the bowl with a towel and put it in a warm place to rise for 16 to 20 hours (an oven, turned off, works great).

Turn out the dough onto a lightly floured

surface. The part of the dough that was flush with the bowl while rising will be the top of the loaf. Shape the loaf by tucking the ragged bottom parts into the center of the loaf — it will look like a belly button. Turn the shaped loaf over, place it back in the bowl, cover it, and let it rise for 2 more hours — it should about double in size.

When you have 45 minutes left of rising time, preheat the oven to 450°F. Wait 15 minutes and then place a heavy lidded pot in the oven. Let it heat up for 30 minutes, then place the bread in the pot, cover it, and let it bake for 30 minutes. After 30 minutes, uncover the pot and continue baking until the bread has a golden, crackly crust, another 15 to 20 minutes.

"The Best Girlfriend You Never Had"

RED FLANNEL HASH

Full disclosure: it was the red flannel hash that led me to Pam Houston, and not the other way around. Rebecca, one of my favorite customers at the butcher shop, frequently comes up to the counter with a basket full of eggs, beets, and potatoes and asks for a pound of thick-cut bacon. It's pretty easy to imagine what could be done with bacon, potatoes, and eggs, but the beets always threw me. When I finally asked her what she was making, her response was one of the loveliest food names I had ever heard: "red flannel hash." The name alone warms you right up.

It is surprising that I had never heard of

red flannel hash, considering I'm a die-hard fan of all forms of breakfast hash. As a kid I went through a Libby's canned corned beef hash phase so intense my mom feared that I would die of salt poisoning. I wanted it on everything — mashed potatoes, chicken, broccoli. I looked for corned beef hash at every restaurant we went to and ordered it stuffed inside an American cheese omelet with a side of buttered white toast. I'm not proud of any of this.

I told Rebecca that I'd never heard of red flannel hash and she said that she had learned about it from Pam Houston's short story "The Best Girlfriend You Never Had." Even more surprising than the fact that I had never heard of red flannel hash is the fact that I had never read any Pam Houston. When *Waltzing the Cat* (the collection of stories that includes "The Best Girlfriend You Never Had") was first published in 1998, my older sister bought a copy of it at a Barnes & Noble because the boots on the cover looked like her Doc Martens.

Coffeehouse culture was still relatively new in 1998, and taking your notebook to a coffee shop to scribble slam poetry or curling up with your impressive, existential novel next to a soy chai was all the rage. The neighborhood Starbucks was the closest thing we had to a cozy, intimate coffee shop, and my sister used to take her copy of *Waltzing the Cat* there and stay for hours, drawing creeping vines and crying girls and scribbling Ani DiFranco lyrics in the book's margins. She was in love with Drew, the barista, who had bored eyes and a safety pin stuck through his left ear, and she was forever hoping that he would ask her what she was reading. Thankfully, he never did because I think she never actually read a word of it, but she turned the book into a piece of her own artwork, a time capsule of her youth and her tireless and hungry quest for love.

The book's narrator, thirty-three-year-old Lucy O'Rourke, is as tireless in her pursuit of love as my seventeen-year-old sister was. Despite myriad fails and countless rejections, Lucy continues to throw herself into destructive relationships, each time falling back on her best friend, Leo, for comfort. The intimacy and comfort between Lucy and Leo is clear from the very first sentence of "The Best Girlfriend You Never Had": "A perfect day in the city always starts like this: My friend Leo picks me up and we go to a breakfast place called Rick and Ann's where they make red flannel hash out of beets and bacon, and then we cross the Bay

Bridge to the gardens of the Palace of the Fine Arts to sit in the wet grass and read poems out loud and talk about love."

Houston, in her minimalist prose, is able to convey volumes — not only about Lucy and Leo's relationship but about Lucy herself — in this one sentence.

In many ways, I'm glad that I didn't read this collection of stories until recently, because I feel that it came to me at precisely the right time (books often seem to do this, don't they?). "The Best Girlfriend You Never Had" is as much a story about romantic and platonic love, love that destroys or heals or consumes, as it is about the love of a place. Much of the story is simply a love poem to San Francisco. In the last year I have lost three of my best friends to San Francisco, each one tiring of New York's snow and grit and grind, and disappearing in a blur to build new lives far away from me. Each of these friends represents a very specific time in my ten years as a New Yorker, and watching them go feels like closing a much-loved chapter of my life here.

When Mo announced to me last spring that she would be moving to San Francisco in only a few days' time, I had just picked up *Waltzing the Cat.* I cried because I would miss her, because I was happy for her, because ten years does feel like quite a long time to be in one place. That night I read "The Best Girlfriend You Never Had" four times.

I found immense comfort in reading about Lucy's budding relationship with her new surroundings, not only because it allowed me to picture more fully the new lives of my friends, but also because it reminded me of my own love affair with New York, and specifically Brooklyn, which is ongoing and everchanging. This place destroys and rebuilds me on a daily — or sometimes even *hourly* — basis, and I am deeply in love with it.

"THE BEST GIRLFRIEND YOU NEVER HAD"

Red Flannel Hash

People are always scared of egg poaching, but fear not — I'm here to show you that it's actually very easy.

Serves 4 generously

   1 1/2 pounds fingerling potatoes, peeled and cut into 1/2-inch cubes

   1 large sweet potato, peeled and cut into 1/2-inch cubes

2 medium beets, peeled and cut into 1/2-inch cubes

1 pound thick-cut bacon, cut into chunks

1 large yellow onion, finely chopped

1 garlic clove, minced

4 thyme sprigs

1/4 cup white vinegar

4 large eggs

Kosher salt

Freshly ground black pepper

Set a steamer basket over a large pot filled with enough water to just reach the bottom of the basket. Place the fingerling potato and sweet potato cubes in the basket and bring the water to a boil over medium heat. Cover the pot and steam the potatoes for 7 minutes. Transfer to a bowl.

Next, steam the beet cubes for 12 minutes. While the beets are steaming, fry the bacon in a cast-iron or other heavy-bottomed skillet over medium heat until lightly crisp. Add the chopped onion and minced garlic and cook over low heat. Once the beets are steamed, add them to the skillet, along with all of the potatoes and the thyme. Cook, stirring occasionally, until the potatoes are crispy, about 20 minutes. Discard the thyme sprigs.

Fill a sauté pan or skillet with water. Add

the vinegar. Heat the vinegar-water over medium heat until very hot, but do not let the water come to a boil, or even to a simmer. You want it to be at that point where bubbles are forming at the bottom of the pan and steam is rising from the surface.

Crack 1 egg into a ramekin and create a whirlpool in the water with a spoon. Gently slip the egg into the water and let it cook for 20 seconds. After 20 seconds you can start very gently nudging the white up around the yolk. If the egg is sticking to the bottom of the pan, just use a spatula to loosen it. Cook for about 3 minutes — the white should look cooked, but you should still be able to see the yolk wiggling around inside. Lift it out with a slotted spoon, place it on a paper towel to drain, season with salt and pepper to taste, and serve on top of the red flannel hash. Repeat with the remaining eggs.

THE SECRET HISTORY
WINE-BRAISED LEG OF LAMB
WITH WILD MUSHROOMS

When I was a little kid, one of my (many) strange and irrational fears was that someday every combination of musical notes would be exhausted and that new music would cease to exist. As a grown-up this is a hard thing for me to explain, which is probably why it was so hard for my parents to understand when I came to them with it. They thought it was just another quirk of mine, and I suppose it was, but I was genuinely terrified. I was in my second year of taking violin lessons when this anxiety emerged; learning to read music had somehow sparked it. My older sister was in her early teens and heavily into radio pop and hip-hop, and I took their repetitive tunes and constant samplings of older songs as proof that my fear was being realized.

In the evenings after school I would spend hours playing records from my dad's collection, which stretched across the entirety of our living room. I found comfort in the Smiths and the English Beat, the Pogues and Dusty Springfield, while I did my homework. By the end of the night, though, I always felt that familiar dread creeping in. It's already all been done, I thought, when I heard Keith Moon's drumming — how could anyone ever do better than this?

Recently, while writing this book, I felt a similar anxiety creeping in. What if someday all of my creative energy just runs out? What if eventually there simply isn't anything left to write about? What if it's all already been done? Put in much simpler terms: I was struggling with debilitating writer's block. In many ways, this is a scary admission, but often I find that saying out loud the things that you are most afraid of somehow makes them seem less scary (unless you finally muster enough courage to say it to your violin teacher and she just stares at you with her mouth agape). In order to admit that you have writer's block you also have to admit that you are *a writer.* This is a terrifying declaration. It feels heavy and self-indulgent and pressure-filled in a way that saying "I'm a butcher" doesn't.

Finally, I admitted all of this to a friend over beers one night. I'm sure she was expecting a much simpler answer to her question, "How's the writing going?" but she listened carefully and responded by telling me about all of the famous writers she had heard about who had suffered terrible creative blocks throughout their careers. The conversation eventually led to Donna Tartt, whose alleged writer's block has generated a good deal of media attention and intrigue since she published *The Secret History* in 1992. The book was an instant bestseller, and people hungrily awaited her next. Eleven years passed between *The Secret History* and *The Little Friend,* and rumors of writer's block–induced breakdowns abounded.

At this point, I had not yet read any Donna Tartt. I think her name always led me to believe that her books would be of the supermarket romance variety (not that there's anything wrong with those). My friend urged me to pick up *The Secret History,* so the next day I went to the bookstore and by the end of the night I had torn through almost the entire book. It's no surprise to me that Tartt had to take eleven years between this book and her next. The anxiety of others' influence is one thing, but I imagine the anxiety of your own influence is quite another. This book must have been a daunting one to follow up.

The book's narrator, Richard, is reminiscent of Charles Ryder from *Brideshead Revisited* — a boy running from his humble beginnings in hopes of making a much more interesting life for himself. He leaves Plano, California, and arrives at the fictional Hampden College in Vermont, where he becomes infatuated with a group of misfit classics students who have isolated themselves from the masses. Henry, Bunny, Charles, Camilla, and Francis spend their days studying ancient Greek with their charming and enigmatic professor, Julian, drinking massive amounts of alcohol, and spending money faster than their parents can make it. After a few short weeks Richard infiltrates the group and quickly finds himself in way over his head.

Things come to a boiling point when Henry, the group's leader, decides that they have to kill Bunny because he knows a secret that could destroy them all (this is given away in the very first sentence, so I haven't ruined anything for you). Henry begins experimenting with poisonous wild mushrooms, trying to determine how many it would take to kill a person Bunny's size. That night, Richard is invited to Julian's house for dinner, and the reader, unsure at this point who in this dysfunctional group can be trusted, watches as Julian presents him with a dinner of roasted lamb and potatoes, leeks and peas with fennel, and lastly, a heaping plate of Henry's wild mushrooms, "steaming in a red wine sauce that smelled of coriander and rue."

The day I finished the book I got an email from the friend who had recommended it. It was a press release stating that Donna Tartt would be publishing a new novel with Little, Brown that year — her third book in more than twenty years. (This, of course, was *The Goldfinch,* which would go on to win the Pulitzer.) When asked what took her so long, Tartt brushed off the rumors of writer's block and unapologetically and succinctly answered, "Writing takes time."

Wine-Braised Leg of Lamb with Wild Mushrooms

Use whatever nonpoisonous varieties of mushrooms you like. I used dried lobster mushrooms, morels, and porcinis and fresh hedgehog mushrooms, yellowfoot chanterelles, and maitakes.

Serves 6

1 (3-pound) bone-in lamb leg steak
Kosher salt
Freshly ground black pepper
5 carrots, peeled and cut into chunks
1 pound fingerling or red potatoes, scrubbed
4 ounces dried mushrooms
1 bunch rosemary
1 bunch thyme
4 cups chicken stock
1 (750-milliliter) bottle dry red wine
10 tablespoons unsalted butter
4 small shallots, minced
4 garlic cloves, minced
8 ounces fresh wild mushrooms
Crusty bread, for serving

Generously season the lamb steak all over with salt and pepper and allow it to sit out until it reaches room temperature, about 40 minutes.

Preheat the oven to 300°F.

Heat a large skillet over medium-high heat and sear the lamb until it forms a nice crust, about 3 minutes per side.

Place the lamb in a Dutch oven and add the carrots, potatoes, dried mushrooms, rosemary, and thyme (reserve a few sprigs of the thyme for cooking the fresh mushrooms). Cover with the chicken stock and red wine.

In the same skillet that you used to sear the lamb, heat 4 tablespoons of the butter over medium heat and add the reserved thyme sprigs. Cook the shallots and garlic until the shallots are translucent — about 8 to 10 minutes. Add them to the Dutch oven, along with 4 more tablespoons of the butter, cut into pieces.

Cover the pot, put it in the oven, and cook until the meat is falling off the bone, about 5 hours.

Strain the stew, reserving the braising liquid. Pick out the herb sprigs and place the meat, potatoes, carrots, and dried mushrooms on a dish.

Place the braising liquid in a medium saucepan and simmer over medium heat until reduced by half, about 20 minutes.

While the sauce is reducing, heat the

remaining 2 tablespoons butter in a sauté pan over medium heat. Add the fresh mushrooms and reserved thyme sprigs. Salt and pepper the mushrooms liberally and cook until they are crisp at the edges and have released most of their liquid.

To serve, spoon the mushrooms into a serving bowl, top with the lamb, carrots, and potatoes, cover in red wine sauce, and season with salt and pepper to taste. Good bread will be necessary for mopping up every last bit.

THE BOOKS IN *VORACIOUS* AND THE RECIPES THEY INSPIRED

Jane Austen, *Emma* • Perfect Soft-Boiled Egg

Jane Austen, *Pride and Prejudice* • White Garlic Soup

Lynne Reid Banks, *The Indian in the Cupboard* • Grilled Roast Beef

Frances Hodgson Burnett, *The Secret Garden* • Currant Buns

Truman Capote, *In Cold Blood* • Cherry Pie

Michael Cunningham, *The Hours* • Birthday Cake

Roald Dahl, *The Witches* • Mussel, Shrimp, and Cod Stew

Tomie dePaola, *Strega Nona* • Black Pepper–Parmesan Pasta

Charles Dickens, *Great Expectations* • Pork Pie

Joan Didion, "Goodbye to All That" • Grilled Peaches with Homemade Ricotta

Daphne du Maurier, *Rebecca* • Blood Orange Marmalade

Jeffrey Eugenides, *Middlesex* • Olive Oil Yogurt Cake

Gillian Flynn, *Gone Girl* • Brown Butter Crêpes

Jonathan Franzen, *The Corrections* • Chocolate Cupcakes with Peppermint Buttercream Frosting

Tana French, *In the Woods* • Chocolate-Covered Digestive Biscuits

William Golding, *Lord of the Flies* • Porchetta di Testa

Jacob and Wilhelm Grimm, "Hansel and Gretel" • Gingerbread Cake with Blood Orange Syrup

Thomas Harris, *The Silence of the Lambs* • Crostini with Fava Bean and Chicken Liver Mousses

Peter Heller, *The Dog Stars* • Whole Roasted Trout

Homer, *The Odyssey* • Red Wine–Rosemary Bread

Pam Houston, "The Best Girlfriend You Never Had" • Red Flannel Hash

Victor Hugo, *Les Misérables* • Black Rye Bread

Washington Irving, "The Legend of Sleepy Hollow" • Buckwheat Pancakes

Carolyn Keene, Nancy Drew • Double Chocolate Walnut Sundae

Ken Kesey, *Sometimes a Great Notion* • Blackberry-Hazelnut Coffee Cake

Harper Lee, *To Kill a Mockingbird* • Biscuits with Molasses Butter

Astrid Lindgren, *Pippi Longstocking* • Buttermilk Pancakes

Robert McCloskey, *Homer Price* • Old-Fashioned Sour Cream Donuts

Herman Melville, *Moby-Dick* • Clam Chowder

Lucy Maud Montgomery, *Anne of Green Gables* • Salted Chocolate Caramels

Toni Morrison, *The Bluest Eye* • Concord Grape Sorbet

Laura Numeroff, *If You Give a Mouse a Cookie* • Brown Butter Chocolate Chip Cookies

George Orwell, *Down and Out in Paris and London* • Rib-Eye Steak

Sylvia Plath, *The Bell Jar* • Crab-Stuffed Avocados

Edgar Allan Poe, "The System of Doctor Tarr and Professor Fether" • Goat Cheese Pumpkin Pie

Wilson Rawls, *Where the Red Fern Grows* • Skillet Cornbread with Honey Butter

Philip Roth, *American Pastoral* • Hot Cheese Sandwich

J. D. Salinger, *The Catcher in the Rye* •
Malted Milk Ice Cream

Maurice Sendak, *In the Night Kitchen* •
Scalded and Malted Milk Cake

Isaac Bashevis Singer, "Gimpel the Fool" •
Challah

Donna Tartt, *The Little Friend* • Peppermint
Stick Ice Cream

Donna Tartt, *The Secret History* • Wine-
Braised Leg of Lamb with Wild Mushrooms

Leo Tolstoy, *Anna Karenina* • Oysters and
Cucumber Mignonette

John Kennedy Toole, *A Confederacy of
Dunces* • Jelly Donuts

Virgil, *The Aeneid* • Honey–Poppy Seed
Cake

Gertrude Chandler Warner, *The Boxcar Children* • Chocolate Pudding

Evelyn Waugh, *Brideshead Revisited* • Blinis
with Caviar

E. B. White, *Charlotte's Web* • Pea and
Bacon Soup

Laura Ingalls Wilder, *Little House in the Big
Woods* • Breakfast Sausage

Virginia Woolf, *Mrs. Dalloway* • Chocolate
Éclairs

ACKNOWLEDGMENTS

This book was the combined effort of many people. Special thanks to my family, who always believed me when I said I would write a book someday: my sisters, Ande and Gemma — the coolest women I know. Cam, my first best friend, Caroline, Jack, Auntie Marcy, Peter, Auntie Sue, Brett (I couldn't have navigated all of those book contracts without you), Auntie Linda. My Papa Seymour, for so much more than I can say here — your unfaltering kindness and positivity, your stories, your warmth, your history. Thank you for teaching me about meat and hard work and generosity. To Lentil, for changing my whole world. To Grandy, I wish you could have seen this. To Emily, for being the bosom friend I always wanted and the sister I chose. Juddy, my sweet, my biggest supporter — thank you for your patience and your love and your fancy dance moves. My Meat Hook family: Ben, Tom,

Brent, Sara, Maddy, James, Mike, David, Gil — I never thought I could love my job or my coworkers so dang much. Harry and Taylor and the Brooklyn Kitchen crew for your knowledge and your willingness to lend me props. To Marion — I am in awe of your talent, thank you for making this book infinitely better. Thank you to all the owners of the various places in the neighborhood who let me make offices in your establishments when I couldn't be in my apartment any longer: the West Café, the Grand, the Second Chance Saloon, Burnside, the Anchored Inn. To Max and Arlo, for letting me watch you grow up and for reminding me what it's like to fall in love with reading. To my Yummy Books readers, who made this book possible — especially you, Elizabeth, my first Internet friend. Kari — super-agent, and Michael — super-editor. To every chef I've worked for, even those of you who threw things at my head and made me feel worthless, you still taught me something. To the people I have toiled beside and for in kitchens and coffee shops throughout NYC: Jason, Willa, Erin, T-shirt, and Mo. To my favorite English teachers, Ms. Jacoby and Mr. Mitchell. To everyone who helped me test these recipes — Mallory and Michelle, my amazing book club girl gang, and so many others. And lastly, to the writers who inspire me every single day and the characters who were my first friends — this book quite literally could not have happened without you.

ABOUT THE AUTHOR

Cara Nicoletti is a butcher, former pastry chef, and author of the literary recipe blog Yummy Books. She comes from a long line of butchers in Boston, Massachusetts, and has been working in restaurants since she moved to New York in 2004. She lives in Brooklyn, teaches sausage making at the Brooklyn Kitchen, and became a butcher at the Meat Hook.

Illustrator **Marion Bolognesi** lives and works in New York City and has exhibited her paintings around the globe. Her website is Marion-B.com.

The employees of Thorndike Press hope you have enjoyed this Large Print book. All our Thorndike, Wheeler, and Kennebec Large Print titles are designed for easy reading, and all our books are made to last. Other Thorndike Press Large Print books are available at your library, through selected bookstores, or directly from us.

For information about titles, please call:
  (800) 223-1244

or visit our Web site at:
  http://gale.cengage.com/thorndike

To share your comments, please write:
  Publisher
  Thorndike Press
  10 Water St., Suite 310
  Waterville, ME 04901